THE
KILLING
OF
JOHN
SHARPLESS

THE
KILLING
OF
JOHN
SHARPLESS

THE PURSUIT OF JUSTICE
IN DELAWARE COUNTY

STEPHANIE HOOVER

THE
History
PRESS

Published by The History Press
Charleston, SC 29403
www.historypress.net

First published 2013

ISBN 978-1-5402-2156-8

Library of Congress CIP data applied for.

Notice: The information in this book is true and complete to the best of our knowledge. It is offered without guarantee on the part of the author or The History Press. The author and The History Press disclaim all liability in connection with the use of this book.

To "My Boys," for whom I wake in the morning.

With deepest gratitude to my family (by blood or circumstance and far-flung as it is), without whose support this book would not be in your hands.

And finally, special thanks to Lynda, who gave me the perfect advice at the perfect time: "Trust the journey." You will never know how much that meant.

Contents

Acknowledgements

Perhaps there are nonfiction writers who can create a book alone from start to finish. I am not one of them. I am, on the contrary, happy to call upon and visit the people and repositories without whom the historical proof this story—and so many others—would be lost.

My sincere thanks go out to the staff of the Delaware County Archives, where both trial documents and the estate records of Susan H. Sharpless were made available to me.

The staff of the Eastern State Penitentiary were invaluable and never failed to return my e-mails. Anyone with even a passing interest in the Pennsylvania prison system (and the famous and anonymous men and women housed within it) should plan to visit this facility, one of the most popular attractions in the Philadelphia area.

The Humanity Gifts Registry, formerly the State Anatomical Board, quietly and respectfully performs a service critical to the health and well-being of the residents of Pennsylvania—many of whom likely aren't even aware of its existence. This nonprofit organization honors the unselfish final donations of individuals and family members, ensuring the dignified recognition that eluded Samuel Johnson.

While more and more of what writers need appears in digital format, the ability to touch "real" records and speak to real experts is one I hope never, ever becomes inconsequential or extinct. I have had the pleasure of working with the same staff members at both the Pennsylvania State Archives and Pennsylvania State Library for a number of years now. No amount of online investigation matches the enjoyment or efficiency of speaking with other humans about your research—especially the very knowledgeable people at these two repositories.

Lastly, my sincere thanks to other writers, researchers and new friends I've met along the way. They cheered me on when I was certain this book would never be finished and—on days when I felt particularly good about myself—reminded me that a manuscript is just a dream until it is delivered to the publisher.

Introduction

I am often asked why I enjoy researching the lives of people who lived generations and centuries before me. To that question, I always offer the same response, which is that I am fascinated at how little humans change. Pages of calendars are torn off and discarded, and one year is inevitably replaced by another—but men, their motives, habits and needs, have and will always remain the same.

Take our fascination with murder, for instance. If offering even the smallest promise of infamy, the victim's former sphere of family, friends, acquaintances and circumstantial bystanders—though they may have no greater relationship than waiting at the same bus stop—will claim intimacy with details only they possess, simply to become part of the story. Police, lawyers and judges whose job it is not just to find the perpetrators but also deliver justice will, if the story is marketable enough, write books about their experiences (with them the stars, of course) or, worse, use their newly minted notoriety to run for some public office. And then there are the members of the media who, having no real skin in the game, work tirelessly to insinuate themselves into the former life of the presently deceased, only to indiscriminately share these personal details with ghoulish enthusiasm. This was as true in 1885 as it is today. It has likely been true since Cain murdered Abel.

News of the killing of John Sharpless was reported across the country, most often in large typeface and bold headlines like the one that caught my attention one day while I scrolled through the pages of a microfilmed newspaper. "A Foul Murder," this particular headline read. Another headline told readers of the "brutal slaughter of an inoffensive Quaker." This was, after all, the time when yellow journalism flourished; Joseph Pulitzer and William Randolph Hearst waged a circulation war, their weapons being the lascivious headlines devised to spur readers into laying down two cents for either the *New York World* or the *New York Journal.* Reporters of that day understood that it was the startling juxtaposition that made the crime so captivating: a pacifist Quaker attacked in his own barn with such force that his skull fractured into pieces. And of course, there were those other elements swirling around the case, coagulating and forming the journalistic equivalent of the weatherman's perfect storm. John Sharpless was a wealthy white man. His accused killer was a poor black man. A widow, sick and further weakened by grief, was the only person who could identify the killer. It was a writer's dream. And then there was the reward...

In the 1880s, no one seemed to realize that the ability of police officers to accept reward money might lead to a conflict of interest. Nor did members of the general public initially seem to mind that the chasing of rewards imbued some police officers with a "quantity not quality" philosophy on arrests. Sadly, the men and women hauled before judges and magistrates based on these myriad questionable arrests had few forms of redress. While the United States Constitution guaranteed the right to assistance of counsel, most courts interpreted this as dependent on whether the defendant *asked* for an attorney. It was only in 1963 that the Supreme Court ruled that states were *required* to provide attorneys to indigent defendants who could not afford them. Before that, most people accused of crimes simply allowed the legal system to operate around them, literally relying solely on the hope that the truth might set them free. Very rarely was any special dispensation made for criminals of low intelligence or obvious mental disability. If convicted, these souls were tossed into the same prisons as murderers, rapists, thieves and thugs who had full control of their minds and actions and easily recognized fellow prisoners who did not.

And so, while I began by saying that people never change, fortunately for all of us, systems do. *The Killing of John Sharpless* is a testament to the fact that the way things are done can always be made better. Be it our legal system, the role of the police, the field of journalism or our wledge of the complexities of human intellectual capability, we now ognize that there is always room for improvement. Unfortunately, this ognition comes well after the late nineteenth century when this crime committed and this case was investigated and tried.

CHAPTER 1

Delaware County Before and at the Time of the Murder

William Penn understood persecution. Even his father opposed his Quaker faith. But when Penn stepped off the ship *Welcome*, he was met by people of similar convictions who had heard of his "great experiment" and wanted to be part of it.

Penn's settlement was preceded by the Dutch, the Swedes and, of course, the original Native American inhabitants who numbered as many as 6,000. Like the Puritans before them, Quakers cast their eyes toward America and viewed it as a place of refuge. By the 1670s, Friends already established in the new country were writing home with news of the peaceful Indians, fertile fields and abundant food. This promise of serenity and wholesomeness urged a large emigration of Quakers, willing to risk anything to escape the unreasonable persecution of their English countrymen to settle in what would become New Jersey, Pennsylvania and Delaware. An estimated 1,400 Quakers awaited Penn's arrival.

The ship *Welcome* left England on September 1, 1682. Two months later, on October 27, Penn made landfall just off the coast of New Castle in what is today the state of Delaware. With him arrived some seventy immigrants. Nearly a third of the passengers died of smallpox on the journey. Two days later, Penn stopped at Upland before proceeding farther north toward Philadelphia. He entered into his labors as proprietor with characteristic vigor and immediately created Pennsylvania's three original counties: Bucks, Philadelphia and Chester. A portion of Chester, including the town by the same name, became Delaware County in 1789.

William Penn's "Great Law" regulating his first three counties was the basis on which the entire commonwealth government eventually operated.

Religious liberty was guaranteed to all. Only indentured servants and vagrants were denied the right to vote. Unlike in England, where the complexity of the law made it difficult for the average person to understand it let alone defend himself, Penn attempted to simplify the legal process for the inhabitants of his new province. The death penalty was abolished for all crimes except willful murder and treason. In his effort to create a perfectly moral state, drunkenness was punishable by fine or imprisonment, as were swearing, lotteries and other "evil" sports and games.

Penn envisioned himself very much as a father to the people of his province. In a proclamation distributed prior to his arrival, he told them:

> *It hath pleased God in His providence to cast you within my lot and care. It is a business that though I never undertook it before, yet God hath given me an understanding of my duty, and an honest mind to do it uprightly. I hope you will not be troubled at your change and the king's choice, for you are now fixed at the mercy of no governor that comes to make his fortune great; you shall be governed by laws of your own making, and live a free and, if you will, a sober and industrious people. I shall not usurp the right of any, or oppress his person.*

Twenty-three vessels arrived in 1682. Most of these immigrants were financially secure. They brought their own furniture, provisions, tools and building supplies, allowing immediate construction of their new homes. But the settlers did not just travel with material goods. The religious tenets and hierarchies established in the old country were reestablished in the new land. Churches performed many of the functions government would later assume: education, relief for the poor and arbitration of neighbors' disputes.

In 1683, some fifty more ships filled with immigrants arrived, most of them Welsh Quakers and Germans whom William Penn had personally invited while sailing the Rhine River. While early German immigrants were Friends, later waves were composed mainly of Mennonites and followers of other faiths. They arrived in the Delaware County region in large numbers and would eventually become a predominant presence in the formerly Quaker landscape.

William Penn's relationship with the Native Americans from whom he purchased land was based on the Quaker principles of fairness and honesty. "Do not abuse them," he said, "but let them have but justice and you win them." While settlers in other states were fighting protracted and bloody battles with native tribes, Pennsylvanians—most of them pacifists and

A 1682 deed of sale from William Penn to John Sharpless for land in Pennsylvania. *Image from* Genealogy of the Sharpless Family.

without weaponry—enjoyed peace, lucrative trade and strong personal friendships. So protective was Penn of the Native Americans with whom he'd negotiated land deals that he made it illegal to sell them alcohol or offer strong drink during the treaty-negotiation process, tactics less scrupulous white bargainers had used to their favor.

Sadly, while Quakers held Native Americans in reverence, they were not—at least in earliest times—averse to the bondage of African Americans. The practice of importing slaves was common from the first days of the province through the early 1700s, when large numbers of Scots-Irish and a second huge wave of German immigrants willingly accepted contracts for as many as seventeen years of indentured servitude in exchange for the opportunity to come to America.

Six decades after Delaware County's inception, 5,280 residents (about a quarter of those answering the question of religion) claimed membership in the Quaker sect. Methodists (primarily German) were quickly gaining a foothold in the county and, with 4,360 members, were the second-largest religious grouping. A much smaller religious sect, those identifying themselves as African Methodists, had only four congregations to the Quakers' sixteen. The African Methodist Bethel Church was organized in the town of Chester on a lot purchased for one dollar from John M. Broomall—close friend to the Sharpless family and a man who figured prominently in Delaware County law and politics.

At the time of the 1840 census, a divided nation and bloody civil rebellion was an unfathomable future horror. Pennsylvania's Quaker leadership had determined more than a century prior that ownership of slaves would preclude members from attaining governance roles. The state legislature, likewise early in its opposition to slavery, passed an edict in 1780 calling for gradual emancipation—an insufficient measure in retrospect but one that preceded the efforts of its neighbors. Under the bill, all children of African Americans born after passage of the law would become free at age twenty-one.

The Civil War devastated the South, and recovery took years. For the North, the postwar period came to be known as America's Gilded Age. Tycoons like Andrew Carnegie and John D. Rockefeller were role models for aspiring millionaires. Trains, both utilitarian and elegant, raced along rails stretching from one coast to the other. The telephone was invented, and the typewriter became *the* high-tech office tool. The United States was a manufacturing goliath.

The financial crash of 1873 abruptly interrupted this period of prosperity. It started in Philadelphia with the closure of the banking house J. Cooke

& Company. Thought to be impregnable, the September 18 run on this esteemed institution set off a national panic. Cooke was invested heavily in the railroads. Overexpansion resulted in the collapse of the bank's credit rating. Account holders demanded withdrawal of their money. Runs on other Philadelphia banks ensued, with the madness soon infecting the entire country. Companies closed, factories ceased production, unemployment skyrocketed and Americans of all economic circumstances suffered a six-year retraction that, until overshadowed by the collapse in 1929, was called the "Great Depression."

By the 1880s, economic recovery was complete and the panic forgotten. Delaware County, like the state and nation at large, was enjoying the second industrial revolution. The *Chester Times* reported that the most exciting events of 1884 were an earthquake and some particularly rancorous political campaigning. Otherwise, people and businesses went about their days in customary fashion.

Expectations for 1885 were bright—and why shouldn't they be? Situated on the Delaware River just southwest of Philadelphia, the residents of Delaware County had survived epidemics, natural disasters, financial loss, harsh Pennsylvania winters and steamy, mosquito-ridden summers. At seventy-five thousand, the population was eight-fold what it had been at the time of the county's formation.

Thanks in large part to the Quaker schools, county children were well educated. Friends believed education led to the knowledge required to aid one's fellow man. But good schools were not the only advantage enjoyed by the people of Delaware County in the late nineteenth century. Its proximity to a major waterway made the area an attractive place to live and conduct business. The waterfront was a lucrative shipbuilding and industrial mecca. Resort hotels sprang up to accommodate the annual influx of urban money. Media's Idlewild Hotel boasted a bowling alley, a nine-hole golf course and a wooden boardwalk leading from the train station to the rear veranda—presumably so its esteemed guests never need soil their expensive shoes on the dusty streets. A stocked pond provided live trout, and a dairy herd supplied fresh milk to the "old Philadelphia families" who arrived at the hotel on the first of May and departed the first of November. Successful business owners, honored military men, great legal minds and important medical pioneers all made permanent homes in the county, adding to its upscale reputation and appeal.

With the Civil War a generation in the past and the county's economy roaring, surely 1885 would be another predictable, peaceful and prosperous year.

CHAPTER 2

The Sharpless Family

Some families possess an innate understanding of their place in history. The fact that they are, and forever will be, a unique aggregate sharing a common bloodline is celebrated from the time of their first family gathering. Early generations of the Sharpless family were like this—preserving family treasures, commissioning written histories and reuniting far-flung cousins from around the country and world.

The first immigrants, John and Jane Sharpless, arrived in Pennsylvania on the ship *Friendship* on August 14, 1682—two months before William Penn's landing. Six of their children arrived with them. The seventh, son Thomas, died on the long voyage from their homeland in England.

To describe these transatlantic trips as arduous is like saying the Revolutionary War was a prolonged skirmish. In a feeble attempt to outwit weather and sea, most ships left England in late summer with the goal of arriving on our eastern coast in early fall. Voyages lasted anywhere from sixty to ninety days. "Ship fever" ran rampant—the seafarer's equivalent of the claustrophobia and restlessness resulting from being pent up in one place for too long. Prevailing winds died suddenly and hid for days. Ships crashed into rocks within sight of their intended ports. Sickness spread as easily as breathing. Survival of every person listed on the passenger manifest was rare. And while some travelers were buried at sea, babies birthed en route took their place in the New World. Knowing these odds, the Sharpless family left the comfortable life enjoyed in their country of birth to come to a place they had never seen to start over—figuratively and literally—from the foundation up.

Sharples Hall in Lancashire, England—the ancestral home of the Sharpless family of Delaware County, Pennsylvania. *Image from* Genealogy of the Sharpless Family.

The family hailed from Sharples in Lancashire, England. Lancashire, located toward the northwestern corner of the country, was founded in the twelfth century. Mention of Sharples is found in very early thirteenth-century records. It was named after a family who once made their home on Sharples Hill, although the last known representative of that clan died in 1816. The ancestral home was beautifully crafted, the archetypal English manor that springs to mind whenever such homes are imagined today. Leaving this place took unimaginable courage.

The family patented three parcels of land in the part of Chester County that would be taken to create Delaware County. These three parcels totaled 870 acres.

Legend has it that after the family settled on their large homestead near Media, they made a ceremonial sacrifice. The family coat of arms—which bears a Latin inscription meaning "suffer bravely for truth"—was buried near a large exposed rock. Onto its face the immigrant John Sharpless carved "1682," along with his initials. The first Sharpless home, a log cabin of sorts built from the surrounding trees, utilized this rock as part of its foundation.

ARMS OF THE SHARPLES FAMILY, 1664.

The Sharpless family coat of arms bearing the Latin inscription *Pro Veritate Suffer Fortiter*, meaning "suffer bravely for truth." *Image from* Genealogy of the Sharpless Family.

From their earliest arrival in what was then Ridley Township, the Sharpless family exercised influence. When rugged, rocky paths made transportation too difficult, it was the Sharpless family who helped petition for new roads. When in 1753 it became "a very Great Inconvenience to meet at the White Horse tavern" to discuss township affairs, the Sharpless family and others successfully lobbied to make Ridley part of the more easily traversable Nether Providence Township.

Four Sharpless men paid taxes to Nether Providence in the 1820s, one of them being John Sharpless Sr., the father of our subject. Between them they owned nearly three hundred acres of township land, the rest of the original patents having been sold off to neighbors and extended family members. These men also owned a fulling mill, gristmill, sawmill, cotton factory, smith shop and blade mill—enterprises constituting a large portion of the township's economy.

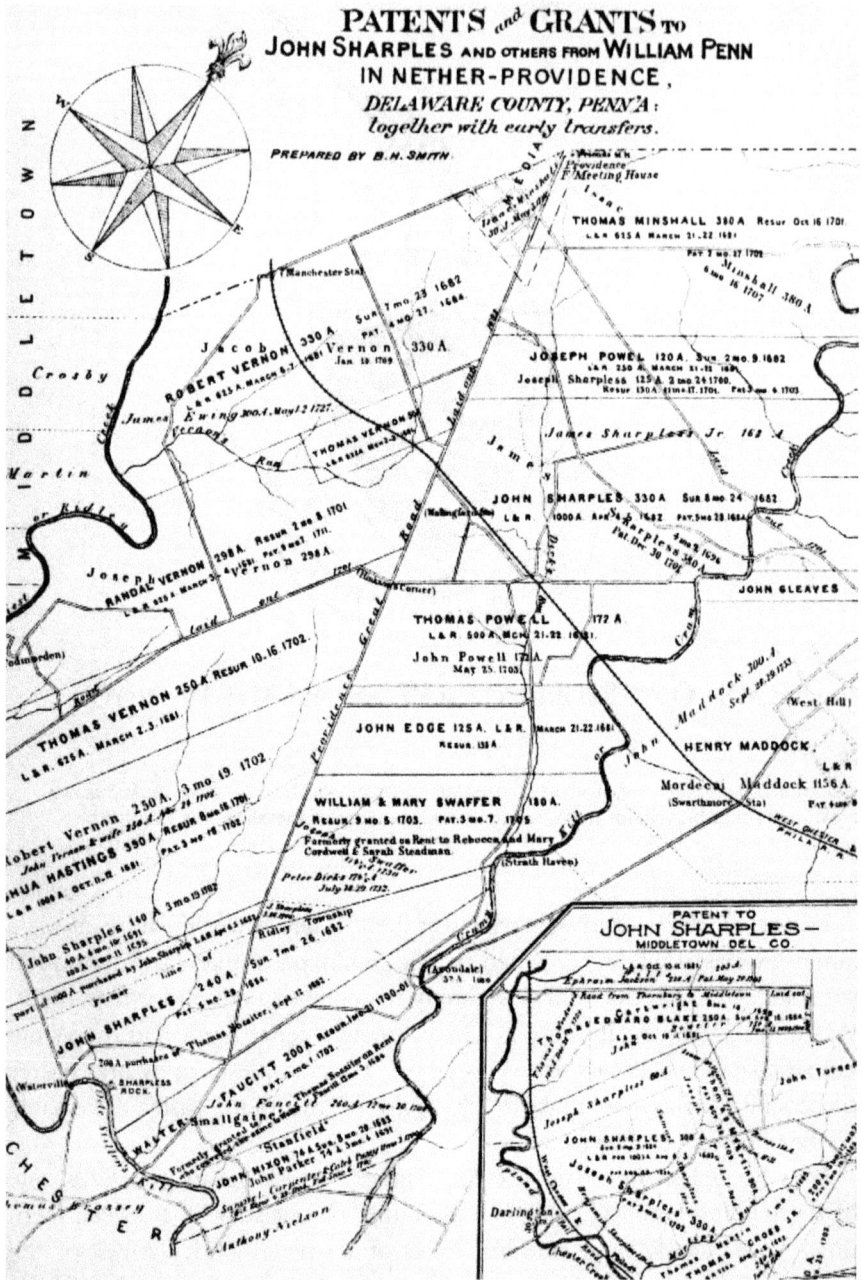

A Nether Providence Township map showing William Penn's patent and grants to John Sharpless and others. *Image from* Genealogy of the Sharpless Family.

An excerpt from the original will of John Sharpless Sr. showing his bequests to son John Sharpless Jr., the subject of this book. *Image created by author from Delaware County court records.*

The John Sharpless who is the subject of this book was born in Nether Providence Township in 1824, a sixth-generation descendant of the immigrant. To distinguish himself from his father (and other family members of the same name), John used the suffix "Junior." Like generations before, his family lived on the acreage first settled by John and Jane Sharpless. It was not a secret that John Sharpless Jr.'s family was wealthy and that this wealth was expected to pass to him and his siblings.

John Sharpless Sr. was born in 1778 while the American Revolution raged. This conflict brought out divisions among Friends. While some Quakers felt inclined to support the fight for liberty, if only by means of supplies and provisions, many others felt such attitudes compromised Friends' pacifist ideals. There are no known records documenting Sharpless family aid to the Revolutionary effort.

John Sr. was a respected member of the Quaker community and in 1816 became an overseer of the Chester Meeting. At his death in 1854, six of his ten children to wife Ruth Martin survived him. He willed his 111-acre homestead to John Jr. Also bestowed to John Jr. was a silver tankard that family lore suggests was brought to America by the original immigrant and lovingly protected by each succeeding generation. To son George, John Sr. gave land that had once been part of the Sharpless farm that he had repurchased.

On November 6, 1856, two years after his father's death, John Sharpless Jr., at the age of thirty-two, took as his wife Susan H. Pratt. Had they married a century earlier, the process would have been a formidable one involving formal consent of not only both sets of parents but also the men and women (separately) of their meetinghouse. By the time of John and Susan's union, the requirements were less arduous.

Quaker marriages were not, legally speaking, civil contracts. "It was the unanimous sense of Friends," said William Penn, "that joining in marriage was the work of the Lord only." This in mind, the parties did not obtain a marriage license but instead resorted to the publication of banns, a public announcement of the couple's intent to wed. By publicizing the intent to marry, anyone recognizing an impediment (knowledge of another spouse, for instance) could speak out. If no objections arose, the couple was free to exchange promises to both live as man and wife until death and to remain faithful members of the Quaker sect.

John Sharpless and Susan Pratt wed in the Springfield Meetinghouse. Although this meeting was established in 1686, the building in which they married was constructed by Orthodox Quakers in 1851—a seemingly simple fact that actually reveals a great deal about who John Sharpless was.

Haverford College, founded in 1833 by Orthodox Quakers, sits partially in Delaware County and partially in Montgomery County. *Image from* A History of Delaware County and Its People.

Though associated with pacifism and tolerance, Quakers found themselves at bitter odds in the 1820s. One group led by Elias Hicks, aptly called the Hicksites, believed their fellow Friends had gone astray. The practice of waiting silently to hear the voice of Christ was being replaced by more mainstream Presbyterian evangelism, they complained. Material pursuits were not shunned but encouraged. Austerity was losing ground in favor of more comfortable living. The divisions became so deep that even two Quaker colleges were established: Haverford, an Orthodox college founded in 1833, and Swarthmore, founded in 1864, which today houses a highly respected collection of Hicksite records.

The Hicksites' criticisms were, on their face, true. Orthodox Quakers were by and large wealthier than their Hicksite counterparts—although evidence of the charity of both groups abounds. Many Orthodox Quakers were "gentlemen" rather than active farmers, meaning they hired out the hard work. Women were, to some degree, dissuaded from ministerial and committee duties in favor of more domestic pursuits.

Silhouette of Elias Hicks, whose followers (the Hicksites) split from the Orthodox Quakers due to disagreements over doctrinal and other issues. *Image from* The Quaker: A Study in Costume.

John Sharpless did not just attend this Orthodox Springfield Meeting; he was also an elder and a member of its Meeting for Sufferings. As in other religious sects, the Friends' term "elder" implies a certain level of wisdom and authority. In the nineteenth-century Quaker church, elders served to ensure

BUILT 1851.

BUILT 1738

John Sharpless and Susan H. Pratt married in the Springfield Meetinghouse, seen here as originally constructed in 1738 and rebuilt by Orthodox Quakers in 1851. *Image from* Genealogy of the Sharpless Family.

that ministers and members conformed to acceptable religious standards. Unquestionably, the Friends in John's community would have recognized and respected his title. As a member of the Meeting for Sufferings, he would also have been known within the Quaker governing hierarchy. Originally tasked with identifying Quakers persecuted and suffering under England's penal system, the Meeting for Sufferings evolved to encompass broader social goals and issues, such as the criminalization of gambling, opposition to war and abolitionist efforts. Service on the Meeting for Sufferings was an important and trusted role and one that required John to travel to the Yearly Meeting in Philadelphia.

John's new wife did not come from wealth, nor was her family involved in Quaker leadership, although they were devout followers. Susan was born in 1825 to Jeremiah Pratt and Ann Hibberd. Jeremiah, a carpenter, nearly erased any chance of the marriage of his daughter to John Sharpless when, in the 1830s, he purchased a farm in Stark County, Ohio. His intent was to move his wife, Susan and Susan's younger sister, Jane, west, but Ann died before his dream was realized.

Although not possessed of an imposing personality, Susan was considered by family and peers to be quite capable intellectually. She was educated at Westtown Friends School in Chester County. This school, which opened in 1799, was the solution to what Philadelphia Quakers viewed as their children's problematic exposure to principles contradicting their religious instruction. As in all things gender-related, Quakers believed in equality of education, so both male and female students of Westtown were taught reading, grammar, penmanship and mathematics. The only skill taught exclusively to young ladies was sewing.

It took more than two years after their marriage, but in February 1859 Susan gave birth to their first and only child. Tragically, Martin P. Sharpless died in March 1863 at just four years, twenty-one days old. Susan had lost her mother as a young girl, so this was the second—but would not be the last—of her inconsolable losses.

Perhaps the timing was coincidental. Or perhaps John and Susan could not bear to remain in the home in which their son had died. Whatever the case, the same year of Martin's death, John erected a new home on the western side of the family's farm, and he and Susan reestablished their household there. The family grew—but not by childbirth. Both Susan's father and her sister, Jane, joined the household. In 1881, Susan buried her father, Jeremiah, who died at ninety-two, an almost unheard-of age for the time.

Photos of the attendees of the Sharpless bicentennial gathering over which John Sharpless presided in 1882. Although taken for inclusion in a book commissioned to celebrate the event, no record exists of the attendees' names. *Images from* Genealogy of the Sharpless Family.

John, meanwhile, had been appointed to preside over an event that surely required at least as much of his time as his church duties: planning the bicentennial celebration of John and Jane Sharpless's 1682 landing. Coinciding with the celebration was the commission of an updated written family history. This assignment went to noted Pennsylvania historian and writer Gilbert Cope.

So many decades had passed since the family first arrived in America. So many challenges, joys, setbacks and accomplishments. Surely John must have pondered his own legacy in light of this history—how would it stand up against the brave, adventurous, faithful ancestors who came before him? What could not be questioned was the success of this momentous reunion, the great attendance of which was even reported in the *New York Times*. Surely John Sharpless hoped to enjoy more such family gatherings. What he did not know, could not know, was that in just three years he would be dead.

CHAPTER 3
Samuel Johnson

Among the many critical decisions faced by nascent American cities was how to house and treat the poor and disabled. England had "poor laws," and these, like many other of its legal precepts, were often adopted and enforced in the new country.

The area now composing the state of Delaware—where Samuel Johnson was born—was originally considered the "lower three" counties of Pennsylvania. As such, it operated under Pennsylvania's laws with regards to aid to the impoverished. Prior to building its first almshouse, the concept of "outdoor relief" was employed. Poor children were outsourced as indentured servants, and anyone accepting assistance was required to wear a red or blue "P," for "pauper," on his or her sleeve. Outdoor relief was phased out in favor of "indoor relief," which simply meant warehousing the poor in homes that often degenerated to criminal detention centers.

By the 1800s, Delaware was fully independent of Pennsylvania's governance and had commenced naming its own local trustees of the poor. Their job was to supervise the construction of housing for the indigent. There was to be one poorhouse per county (three in total), and admittance was based on the approval of two trustees. As in Pennsylvania, costs of operating this poorhouse system were raised by tax levies. Soon the use of these funds—and the efficacy of the poorhouse system in general—were being questioned.

"No burden is so oppressive to the people of this state, as the support of our present poor house system." This statement, part of a message from

Governor Charles Thomas to the Delaware House of Representatives, was delivered in 1824. The governor went on to express his concerns about whether the poor were receiving nurturing assistance or an education in vice. And he wondered aloud if the services provided might actually be weakening the resolve of the poor to improve on their current circumstance.

Within a few years of the governor's letter, new regulations appeared, some unimaginable by modern society. Unmarried "negro or mulatto" women giving birth to "bastard" children while taking asylum in a poorhouse were required to provide three years of servitude to the state—nearly twice the previously required eighteen months. Terms of this service were to be considered the same as those between "master and servant," according to state statutes. Families with means to pay for the care of their indigent relatives were required to do so. Legislation also mandated that corporations or entities (such as those constructing the Chesapeake and Delaware Canal at that time) accept liability for any immigrants or employees added to the Delaware poor relief system.

In 1849, the Delaware legislature determined that poorhouses were to be called "almshouses"—a subtle distinction, perhaps, to insinuate that the public at large should donate (give alms) toward care of the indigent rather than making this an obligation of government. By the 1850s, the poor "house" was replaced by a poor "farm," on which residents were required to work, if able. Gradually, farms evolved into two separate entities, workhouses and asylums for the insane, the latter of which was the precursor to the state and county hospital system that, in the twentieth century, assumed care for the aged, impoverished and disabled.

It was in the New Castle County poorhouse in Wilmington that Alexander, aka Cuff, aka Samuel Johnson was born about 1849. His mother, we can assume, was one of those African American women destined to spend three years in servitude to the state in exchange for the privilege of giving birth in this institution. We do not know if she was a slave, although—as evidenced by slave schedules created as part of Delaware's 1850 census—the state's economy was far less reliant on this forced labor than its neighbors to the south.

Johnson's mother, for reasons we do not know, turned care of her child over to his grandparents. In 1869, he left his grandparents' house for Newark, Delaware, where he worked as a farmhand for several years. From Newark, he moved to Elkton, Maryland, where his career as a petty thief fully blossomed. About 1879, after serving a jail sentence, he left Elkton and moved thirty-five miles north to Chester, Pennsylvania.

By today's measure, Johnson would not be considered a large man, but in the 1880s the average male height was about five feet, six inches. At the age of forty, Johnson stood five feet, nine inches tall. By boxing standards, his 152-pound body would now be considered only slightly larger than welterweight. Compared to his contemporaries, however, he would have appeared dominating.

Johnson apparently never learned a specialized skill or trade. His occupation—laborer—implies that he likely took the hard jobs no one else wanted when and where he could find them.

Samuel Johnson lacked the benefit of choice. His life was dictated by the circumstances of his birth, and he never surmounted them. Johnson was described on prison intake records as "intemperate," meaning he, on occasion, got drunk. Throughout his life, he was described as intellectually challenged. Impairment accompanied by illiteracy no doubt muted his recognition of what was right and wrong. Johnson's motives were basic: he took what he needed to survive. None of his crimes—accused or tried—prior to 1885 involved violence.

Johnson never gave a clear answer as to his whereabouts on the evening of November 22, 1885. Like all vacuums, this one would be filled, but unfortunately for Johnson, its contents would be the recollections of others not mindful of his best interests.

CHAPTER 4
The Murder

At eight thirty on Sunday evening, November 22, 1885, the thermometer in the town of Chester registered forty-two degrees, typical for that time of year. What drove the people of Delaware County inside to their warm fires was not just the chill but also the heavy rain and howling winds that came with it. It was the kind of weather felt in the bones.

The Sharpless home sat at the end of a long, private lane. It was a handsome, two-story residence with eleven rooms (including a bathroom), hot-water heat and a mansard roof. Also on the property were a double-decker barn, a stone stable for a large dairy operation, a carriage house, a springhouse and a smaller wooden house where servants lived. The home was surrounded by tall, mature trees and a substantial orchard.

John sat by a lamp reading. Susan was writing. Her cousin Lydia Reynolds was conversing with Susan's sister, Jane M. Pratt. The last thing they expected to hear was rapping on the front door. Who would be out in this weather?

John, as was his habit, swung open his door without hesitation. He saw a man standing some distance from the threshold. "What does thee want?" he asked. The ladies could hear the ensuing conversation but couldn't decipher the content. After several moments, Jane went to see who had come to the home on such an inclement night. John explained that a carriage had broken down out on the road and that this caller had come asking for assistance with the repair.

"Do you know this man?" she asked.

"No," John replied.

John Sharpless, born in 1824 on the family homestead in Nether Providence, Delaware County. He was murdered there in 1885. *Image from Genealogy of the Sharpless Family.*

While John was gathering his hat, coat, lantern and umbrella, Jane went to the door to see the caller for herself. "Is anyone hurt?" she asked the stranger. He said he did not know for he was not part of the group riding in the carriage—he had only come upon them while walking the road.

Jane was leery and confused and could not quite see the face of the man at the door. She asked John if the caller was a white man or a black man, to which John replied, "No, he is a white man."

Perhaps it was intuition or just a natural response to the cold, dark night and its driving rain and wind. Whatever prompted it, Jane asked John not to leave with the stranger but rather give him some supplies kept in the house. John declined her suggestion and said he was taking the man to the barn to find what he needed to fix the wagon. She watched John head off into the rain, the stranger following behind. Jane returned to the sitting room.

Some thirty minutes passed with no sign of John's lantern approaching the house. Susan, who was ill, became increasingly alarmed and agitated. Jane, no doubt hoping to assure both her sister and herself that all was well, donned her coat and rubbers (waterproof overshoes) and walked down the long, dark lane and out to the road to learn John's whereabouts. Finding no sign of a wagon, the stranger or her brother-in-law, she returned to check the barn.

Just in front of the door lay John's umbrella.

BACK AT THE SHARPLESS home, Susan and Lydia waited and worried. They heard the front door latch rattle and were surprised and frightened to see a tall black man enter the sitting room. Susan rose to meet him. "What does thee want?" she asked the stranger.

"I want a little money," he answered.

"We are not in the habit of keeping money in the house," Susan explained, but the stranger was insistent. "But I want some," he said.

Susan did not answer, and in the silence the man looked about the room. He asked if there was a young girl living in the house. Susan asked if he meant a young black girl, but the man said, "No, a white girl."

Thinking he meant the young servant girl in their employ, Susan responded bravely, "We do but thee cannot see her. She is not our daughter, and thee cannot see her."

Lydia now spoke up and told the man there was a black family living on the property. She suggested he may want to speak to them and said she would call them. The stranger replied that he did not want to see that family and began backing out of the room, casting glances back and forth between the women, the sitting room window and the front door. When the women heard the door latch behind him, they quickly ran to bolt him out.

IF THE STRANGER SAW Jane as he left the Sharpless house, he did not approach her. She, alone, stood outside the barn calling for her brother-in-law.

"John?" Jane shouted.

Hearing no answer, she called again: "John?"

After a third unanswered call, she picked up John's umbrella and ran to the nearby home of Joseph E. Mickel. He and his brother William were about to leave in their carriage when Jane arrived, panicked. She quickly described the events of the evening, and the trio rushed back to the Sharpless stable. All three went inside. All three instantly knew that John Sharpless was dead.

He must have been struck on the back of the head the moment he stepped inside the barn. The blow was devastating. It was delivered with sufficient strength to fracture the Quaker's skull into several pieces. John fell forward after the strike, landing with his feet just inside the barn and his head near the horse stall. John's hat, which lay near him, was bloodstained. The coroner—whom, along with the police, William Mickel had summoned—thought the weapon might have been the blunt end of a hatchet.

By the time Delaware County chief of police Williamson (his first name has been lost to history) arrived, all three women knew that John Sharpless was dead. Susan descended into hysterics. Jane and Lydia were not much more composed than Susan. With persistence born out of practice, Williamson teased a description out of his three witnesses: about five feet, ten inches, maybe 160 pounds; a smooth face, almost giving the appearance of a mask; either a black man or a white man made up to look like one; prominent teeth; unusual manner of speaking; dark clothes and soft hat; white handkerchief around his neck. It was enough of a description on which to base a search of the surrounding area. But as the men were organizing to do just that, flames appeared at the nearby Lindsay farm. Neighbors rushed to help save the structure, but they were defeated by the inferno, which destroyed the entire fall harvest and the livestock housed within.

Did the murderer set the barn alight knowing it would prevent a manhunt? Chief Williamson thought so. But he had another means of letting the surrounding communities know about the awful crime in Nether Providence Township. Within hours, telegrams were sent to police departments telling them to be on the lookout for the man who killed Quaker John Sharpless of Delaware County.

NEWS OF THE MURDER of one of the county's most respected citizens spread quickly, not only in mainstream newspapers but also in Quaker publications. The *Friend* reported the murder and also ran an obituary:

Humility and watchfulness and a low estimate of his own attainments were very conspicuous traits in the character of our beloved friend and were evinced by his daily prayerful and careful walk before the world. In a letter to a friend written but three days before his death these virtues were strikingly manifested by the following language: "My earnest desire is to know more of that purifying work which it is needful for all to submit to cleanse the heart from the defilements of sin and bring it into closer union with the loving spirit of the dear Saviour, and that my feet may be kept in the narrow way the few remaining days of my life is the sincere prayer of my heart."

Although death came at an unexpected moment yet his family and friends, while deeply afflicted, are comforted in the assurance that it is well with him and that through mercy his immortal spirit has been permitted to enter into endless bliss.

"Mark the perfect man and behold the upright, for the end of that man is peace."

This same publication also reflected on Samuel Johnson:

It is one of the consolations of the Lord's servants that whatever accidents may befall them, the everlasting arms are underneath and all things shall work together for good to them that love Him. But how inexpressibly pitiful is the condition of the miserable murderer and what a cruel taskmaster does Satan prove to those who become his servants.

John's will was probated nine days after his murder. It was a short, simple document written twelve years previously. He gave all real estate and personal property—after payment of his debts and funeral expenses—to his wife, Susan H. Sharpless, and her heirs. There was no specific mention of the silver tankard passed down from previous generations and therefore no instructions for a future caretaker.

The funeral was held on Thanksgiving and was astounding in attendance. The *Chester Times* called it one of the largest funerals to take place in the history of the county. More than three hundred carriages arrived in advance of the ceremony, most of the drivers and passengers easily identified by their wardrobes as Quakers. More attendees arrived on foot.

An estimated 1,200 people shuffled past the plain coffin on view in the home. No fewer than 8 persons eulogized John Sharpless before his pallbearers lifted his casket onto a waiting horse-drawn hearse, which took it to the cemetery. He was buried beside his parents and little son, Martin.

As the solemn attendees dispersed, their attention was drawn to a wild, sobbing man who flung himself at the fresh grave. An officer of the North Chester Police restrained the stranger and demanded to know the meaning of his actions. The man, who called himself John Evans, purported to be a reporter from Philadelphia who came to investigate the murder. He thrust papers into the officer's hand, an attempt to substantiate his story. Seeing that these contained nothing of decipherable content, the officer arrested Evans and placed him in the Media jail. After some investigation, it was determined the man was insane. Apparently, he had been drawn to the area by the publicity surrounding the murder, about which he advised, "Look in the axe factory and all will be discovered." On the chance that the claim contained some small kernel of validity, the factory was searched. Nothing was found.

CHAPTER 5

The Investigation

There is an old expression that says the fish rots from the head down—a colorful way of stating that if the head of an organization is corrupt, chances are his underlings are as well. The head of the Philadelphia Police in 1885 was Mayor William Burns Smith. Born in Scotland in 1844, Smith was a jovial, personable man and one who could easily influence those around him. He was known somewhat pejoratively as the "Dandy Mayor"—a nod to his expensive, fanciful wardrobe.

In Smith's April 1884 inaugural address, he specifically addressed his goals for the police department:

> *The establishment of a police force which will protect life and property and secure the fearless execution of the laws will greatly rest upon the organization and the discipline demanded. I shall devote to the service the best of my energies and judgment. The selection of those appointed shall be dictated by a desire to secure the best men attainable for the force, and no influence shall prevent the dismissal of those who, by any action or negligence, shall fail to perform their whole duty. Promotion shall be the reward of faithful service, and commanding officers shall be required to exact discipline and enforce their authority, and no requirement shall be exacted except that of honestly and fidelity.*

Sixteen months into his term, Mayor Smith was contacted by the city controller. Receipts showed Smith had collected $8,000 in revenue for the city—mostly from fees paid for pawnbroker, theatrical, gunpowder and coal oil licenses—but he had forwarded only $2.50 to the controller's office. Although Smith eventually supplied the full amount indicated by the receipts, the circumstances of the repayment led the suspicious controller to request an audit of the mayor's records. The books presented to the auditors "appeared not to be books of original entry, but bore the marks of recent

Lieutenant David B. Roche was one of the Philadelphia police officers responsible for the arrest of Samuel Johnson. His career would end after one of his own violent outbursts. *Image from* The Philadelphia Police, Past and Present.

preparation." Worse, Mayor Smith declined to provide the deposit and check books associated with the city account.

The revelations of Smith's mismanagement of city funds proved insurmountable, and in September 1886, articles of impeachment were filed against him. In addition to the financial irregularities, Smith was accused of being so derelict in overseeing the police department that his special officers could not provide sufficient evidence of service to even justify receipt of their salaries.

Two of Smith's most widely recognized Philadelphia policemen would make regular visits to the Sharpless farm: Lieutenant David Roche and Special Officer Thomas Alexander. The duo possessed the most suspect and prolific arrest records that the Philadelphia Police Department had ever seen. Roche, who was barely into his teens when he enlisted to serve as a drummer boy for the Union army, first witnessed the carnage one man can inflict on another at an early age. As an adult, his propensity for violence, no doubt fueled by copious amounts of alcohol, was well known. Alexander started his police career as a patrolman and was promoted to special officer just three years later. Over the course of his career, he made 610 arrests, with nearly 100 of those prisoners serving sentences at the notorious Eastern State Penitentiary. Like Roche, Alexander was a tough customer. During one arrest, his unwilling detainee stabbed him seven times with a butcher knife, wounds from which Alexander completely healed.

At the time of the Sharpless investigation, police officers were as eligible as the general public to collect rewards for the capture of those suspected of crimes. And it was no secret that the effort exerted in the search for criminals often correlated to the size of the reward offered. Immediately after the murder, both the Sharpless family and the Delaware County commissioners posted $500 rewards. One thousand dollars was a huge incentive in 1885—in fact, it was more than twice what the average resident of the county earned in a year. Whether Roche and Alexander worked the Sharpless murder for the fame, the reward or both, they became familiar faces near Media. But they weren't the only Philadelphia police officers busying themselves with the case.

The day after the killing of John Sharpless, the police of Philadelphia's Twenty-third District arrested Isaac Lewis, a "negro answering the description" of the murderer. He was arraigned on November 24 and shortly thereafter released when it was proven he was nowhere near the Sharpless farm. But while Lewis was being released, officers from other Philadelphia precincts arrested three more men, only to grudgingly free them when alibis or

Map of the Nether Providence Township showing John Sharpless's land bordering John Lindsay's land (lower left corner). *Image from* Combination Atlas Map of Delaware County.

failures in identification ruled them out. Not to be outdone, the police of Delaware County were arresting anyone who acted the least bit suspiciously or bore the tiniest resemblance to the description given by Susan H. Sharpless and her sister and cousin.

As if interest in the case were not already overwhelming, the telegrams Chief Williamson sent to neighboring police departments were picked up by the Associated Press, which distributed news of the murder nationwide. Dozens of morbidly curious people toured the murder scene, slopping through the mud that the continuing rain now deepened. It must have been a surreal scene for the widow, whose illness only worsened with grief. Susan watched as investigators (some local, many not), amateur detectives and strangers of every ilk trampled her beautiful homestead. Nearby, the Lindsay barn still smoldered, and the unpleasant odors of charred wood and burnt livestock traveled for miles.

DR. FRANK ROWLAND and his son completed the autopsy on John Sharpless. As was first assumed, when they removed the scalp, they found that the skull was crushed as though hit by the blunt, small face of a hatchet.

Some speculated that the murderer was still hiding in the community. Searches were conducted—some police-sanctioned, others by private citizens—but there remained confusion as to what the suspect actually looked like. Was he black? White? A white man who darkened his face as a disguise? Who could tell by Susan's vague description. The only thing clear was that the lure of reward money meant any African American man unfortunate enough to be found within one hundred miles of the Sharpless home might be grabbed by police—or an overzealous bounty hunter. It was an "arrest now, ask questions later" approach, and it proved one thing: no one suspect could as yet confidently be called the killer.

I. Preston Thomas, a successful Philadelphia phosphate manufacturer, went one step further than most would-be private investigators. When James Edward Page showed up at Thomas's office seeking work, Thomas had his men detain Page while he went to the Delaware County Courthouse to tell district attorney Jesse M. Baker that he had captured the killer of John Sharpless. Constable Jesse Hoopes accompanied Thomas back to his office and arrested Page, who said he was from "the South" and had only come looking for a job. At five feet, eight inches and about 160 pounds, his build comported with the intruder's description, but a local newspaper reporter said his face bore no resemblance whatsoever. Like the others, Page was released.

Thanksgiving 1885 fell on November 26. Four days had passed, and the citizens of Delaware County were beginning to doubt that the murderer would be captured. Divergent theories circulated in taverns, stores and churches. Did an escaped lunatic kill John Sharpless? Norristown Hospital was contacted but reported no unaccounted inmates. John Lindsay discovered only three charred skeletons of horses in his barn rather than the four housed there. Had the murderer used the missing horse for his getaway shortly after the murder? Is this why searches of the woods and nearby farms proved futile?

Chief Williamson started to feel the pressure that comes with unsolved cases of high public interest. The reward had risen to an astounding $2,000. This escalated the appearance of self-appointed detectives who scoured the countryside, stiff canes and heavy clubs in hand. Hearing that the Philadelphia police were coming to Delaware County to arrest a man named John Carpenter, Williamson sped off in the middle of the night to capture the suspect first. Meanwhile, a coal and iron policeman from Valley Forge was equally confident that he had earned the reward. On the same day that Williamson threw Carpenter in the Media jail, this man brought a mulatto named Brown for Susan's identification.

For any suspect to be tried and convicted of killing her husband, Susan would have to positively identify him as the man who had entered her sitting room the night of November 22. Family counsel and ex-judge John M. Broomall knew that. The police knew that. Most importantly, perhaps, Susan herself knew that. Unable to leave her home due to sickness, the two latest suspects, Carpenter and Brown, were taken to her. What transpired was sheer theater.

While Broomall, Coroner Fairlamb, Lydia and Jane watched, the shutters were clasped and the room darkened. Lamps were lit and arranged as they had been the night of the murder. With the scene properly set, Susan entered the sitting room with Dr. Rowland supporting her on one side and Henry Palmer on the other. After what must have seemed an eternity, Chief Williamson instructed Carpenter to enter the front door and proceed to the sitting room. Carpenter reenacted the intruder's steps perfectly.

Susan barely retained her composure as the man approached. Somehow she mustered the strength to rise and stand before the stranger, exactly as she had done the night of the murder. Time passed, but Susan made no judgment. She sat and stood three more times, each time coming a bit closer to Carpenter, each time taking in more of his look, his attitude. She studied every aspect of Carpenter's physicality—his demeanor, his posture, his scent.

After rising and appraising him for the fourth time, she collapsed into her chair. "Take him away," she told Williamson. "I must sleep."

Whether she lacked the energy to stand or instead decided to wait to regain the strength to continue, Susan remained in her chair. Meanwhile, Williamson asked Jane Pratt if this was the man she'd seen leave with her brother-in-law. "He bears a striking resemblance," she replied, to which Lydia agreed.

Susan was determined to make one final attempt at identification. Once again, she rose and moved toward Carpenter. To no one in particular she announced that he made her feel the way the intruder had, frightened and uncomfortable—but this did not mean Carpenter was the same man. While Susan stood in proximity, Carpenter was asked to say, "I want a little money. I must have money." He did so. Susan listened intently. She watched his mouth as he spoke.

"Is that the man?" Chief Williamson asked.

Susan dropped back down into her chair before answering. "I cannot be sure," she said.

Brown waited nervously outside the home. When Carpenter finally emerged, he was led inside. Susan's immediate dismissal brought equal shares of relief for him and disappointment for the group from Valley Forge that was already planning how to spend the substantial reward.

Without Susan's positive identification, John Carpenter assumed he would be released and sent home to his wife. Instead, Williamson returned him to the lockup, where Carpenter somehow found and retained attorneys James S. Cummins and George E. Darlington.

Some newspapers proclaimed Carpenter a guilty man. Others felt he was being railroaded by Williamson because no other likely suspect had been found. The *Chester Times* voiced the thoughts many residents of Delaware County now spoke only in private: Susan would never identify any man as the murderer for she could not—would not—be responsible for a hanging.

Try as he might, Chief Williamson could find no witness to contradict Carpenter's story that he spent the day of the Sharpless murder in church and that evening at home with his family. All the while, Williamson was receiving telegrams from other police departments assuring him that they had the *real* killer of John Sharpless in custody. The chief in Syracuse, New York, sent a dispatch saying he was holding a man with a broad English accent and four fingers missing from his right hand—"What should we do with him?" "Let him go," came Williamson's reply. Wilmington, Delaware's chief John J. Dougherty assured Williamson that the suspect in his jail either killed Sharpless or was guilty of some other crime judging by his nervous demeanor. Williamson replied that this man, too, should be released. A Maryland police chief caused a brief stir with his telegram, which declared, "I have arrested the colored man who murdered John Sharpless." A complete lack of resemblance to the man described by Susan earned this prisoner his fast release. And cops weren't the only ones making hasty decisions. A newspaper in Philadelphia ran what it claimed to be a sketch of murder victim John Sharpless taken from a recent photograph only to later learn that it was actually a drawing of a bishop from Georgia.

Even with Carpenter in jail and more arrests announced daily, the citizenry was not satisfied with the investigation. It was becomingly increasingly clear that the reward money had done far more harm than good. John M. Broomall shared publicly his doubts about the guilt of John Carpenter, adding that Susan Sharpless felt the same. It was no secret that, like the Quaker Sharpless family, Broomall abhorred capital punishment.

A new theory now floated from neighbor to neighbor, pew to pew and tavern to tavern. Supposedly, shortly before the murder, a band of gypsies was encamped on the Sharpless farm—something John was not happy about. Couldn't a gypsy be confused with a colored man, especially at night? Maybe they were angry with John for running them off. Maybe it was a gypsy who killed John Sharpless. Although it made for interesting speculation, the idea was soon dismissed.

On December 2, after spending seven days in jail on no real evidence, John Carpenter was sent home. The streets were lined with African American men celebrating this release. As Carpenter left the lockup with his wife and several friends, he was congratulated and celebrated by the assembled crowd. "You're better known today than you were a week ago," one man was overheard exclaiming. Although reveling in this bit of notoriety, Carpenter made an attempt to sound conciliatory. Of the cops who arrested him, he proclaimed, "I know you were after that big money, and as I answer the description in some respects, I cannot well blame you." But, he added, the attitudes of the police between the day of his arrest and the day of his release were drastically different. It was "Mr. Carpenter when I was released," he said. "The other day it was 'the nigger.'"

On the same day that Carpenter was set free, Lewis Morris Lewis, who lived seven miles from the Sharpless home, reported an interesting visit, one he had not shared with police earlier because he had not heard of the murder until days after it occurred. On the morning of November 23, a man had appeared at his door asking for food. He said he'd been traveling since midnight. He was wet and hungry. He wore a long coat, was broad shouldered and stood about five feet, ten inches tall. After they fed him and the stranger left, Lewis noticed that his coat was missing. A well-worn one was left in its stead. He did not know if this was helpful but thought the police should know.

On December 4, another $1,000 was added to the reward money, this from the police journal *American Police Record*, which enjoyed nationwide distribution. Two days later, with no new clues or suspects surfacing, the story of the murder all but disappeared from the newspapers.

It came roaring back to the headlines just before Christmas. That was when Lieutenant David Roche and Special Officer Thomas Alexander arrested Alexander "Cuff" Johnson, alias Samuel Johnson, in Philadelphia for the killing of John Sharpless.

CHAPTER 6
The Arrest

By the first week of December 1885, the citizens of Delaware County were convinced the Sharpless murder would go unsolved. No weapon turned up at the farm or in the surrounding woods, and these areas were searched time and time again. Brief excitement followed the discovery of a brick with a string tied around it, but any hope of it becoming a new clue was quashed when children claimed it as a toy. People reminded themselves of the last man hanged in Delaware County, a killer apparently destined to keep that distinction. The only way the murderer of John Sharpless would be caught, it was thought, was if he confessed. Or if someone turned him in.

Samuel Johnson was released from Moyamensing Prison on November 20, 1885, after serving eight months for a larceny conviction. Moyamensing—also known as Philadelphia County Prison—was one of the correctional institutions built on what became known worldwide as the Pennsylvania model: solitary confinement and hard labor. It was designed by noted architect Thomas Ustickle Walter, who also designed the dome atop the United States Capital, as well as its House and Senate wings. When construction concluded in 1835, Moyamensing was meant to hold four hundred prisoners. Debtors were to be housed in a separate wing of the prison, but laws abolishing debtors' prison were passed shortly after Moyamensing opened so that purpose was never fulfilled. Located about two miles outside Philadelphia's city center, Moyamensing's imposing three-story façade was made of Kennebunk granite. Convicts were taught trades that they performed in their nine- by eleven-foot cells, the most oft-learned being spinning, weaving and shoemaking. The most extreme offenders received only water and a half pound of bread each day. A 1901 report described Moyamensing as a modern marvel, "scrupulously clean and in order everywhere." Coal-fed furnaces supplied steam heat throughout, and inspectors spoke quite highly of the prison's electric plant, which generated "sufficient voltage for an electrocution-chair" should that method be preferred over the gallows. The biggest problem Moyamensing and other prisons faced was how to separate those already convicted from the arrested but untried inmates who sometimes waited years for their days in court.

Just three days after his release from Moyamensing, Johnson was back in jail based on the statements of his wife and acquaintances, whose stories, according to police, proved his complicity in the murder of John Sharpless.

Samuel Johnson's relationship with Mollie Stevens was both murky and temporary. She called herself his wife, and Johnson considered himself the father of her child. In all likelihood, however, the marriage was common law. Mollie was squat and unkempt and prone to scowling. She was also a thief in her own right. Whether she learned this from Johnson or their shared hobby brought them together, we do not know. We do know that to Mollie and her friends, the $3,000 in reward money now being offered for the capture of the killer of John Sharpless was a fortune.

Today, thanks to its countless repetition on weekly court dramas and police procedurals, nearly everyone can recite the Miranda warning by heart: "You have the right to remain silent. Anything you say can and will be used against you in a court of law. You have the right to an attorney. If you cannot afford an attorney one will be appointed to you." It is therefore easy to forget that Miranda rights are a recent development in our trial system. In fact, recitation of Miranda rights has been required only since 1966. At the time of Samuel Johnson's arrest, the police were under no obligation to offer such warnings, nor did the court system offer to provide a defense lawyer—another legal protection established in the 1960s. During Johnson's December 22 arraignment on the charge of murdering John Sharpless, the prosecuting attorney was present, but Johnson was responsible for his own defense. To his credit, Magistrate Smith did caution Johnson against saying anything self-incriminating, although what, if anything, Johnson knew of that concept is debatable.

By 1:30 p.m., when the arraignment began, the small hearing room was packed with spectators who seemed to arrive out of nowhere. Four policemen were called in to control the crowd and keep the passageway to the magistrate's office clear. Johnson was led into the room at two o'clock.

In response to Magistrate Smith's questions, Johnson said he lived with Carrie Lane and took farm work or any other jobs he could find. He said he understood he was being charged with murder.

Special Officer Thomas Alexander was the first witness called, and he testified to arresting Samuel Johnson on the basis of information received about Johnson's confession to the crime. That information, he said, came from Mollie Stevens. What did not come out in this or subsequent hearings were the threats of physical harm Alexander leveled at Stevens to persuade her to speak.

The next witness to testify, and the ex-con on whose testimony prosecutors almost solely relied, was Alexander Pritchett. Pritchett's story was both interesting and fluid. During the arraignment, he explained that he knew Johnson from Moyamensing. Pritchett had been incarcerated for assault and battery. Johnson was serving time for stealing chickens. This being late fall, Pritchett said the two men struck up a conversation about going to New York for Christmas—a reasonable plan for anyone possessing an appreciation for culture and a propensity for adventure. After all, by the 1880s, the city was well associated with the holidays. Merchants bathed shop windows with festive garland and gift ideas. Children clamored to see the newest toys and games. Thomas Nast, the famous caricaturist and *Harper's Weekly* cartoonist, provided the first universal vision of Santa Claus, and it seemed to appear everywhere in the city. Whether two uneducated convicts were savvy enough to recognize these newborn cultural and holiday rituals is unclear, but neither the magistrate nor Johnson questioned the story.

All that was needed to make the New York trip was, of course, money—but Pritchett said Johnson viewed that as a minor obstacle. He knew where to get two or three hundred dollars when he got out.

Pritchett was released from Moyamensing on October 22 and told Johnson to meet him at Seventh and Lombard when he, too, got out. In what could be described as an incredible act of synchronicity, a month later the two men appeared on this exact corner, on the exact same day, at the exact same time.

On that fortuitous Friday, November 20, Pritchett testified that he and Johnson went for drinks. On Saturday afternoon, they met again and drank at a nearby tavern until after midnight. This was corroborated by Special Officer Alexander, who had earlier testified to seeing them there.

At one o'clock in the morning on Sunday, November 22, 1885, Samuel Johnson—after just being released from one of the harshest prisons in the nation and after drinking for two days with very little sleep in between—told Pritchett he was heading to "the country" to secure his stake for the New

York trip. The unsuccessful Johnson returned to Philadelphia several days later to tell Pritchett that he had killed a man near Chester by knocking him on the head. After killing the man, Pritchett testified, Johnson said he took six dollars and a knife from his pockets.

Magistrate Smith interrupted Pritchett's testimony to ask Johnson if he had anything to say about the story. "It's not true," Johnson replied. He admitted to seeing Pritchett after being released from Moyamensing, but Johnson asserted that it was Pritchett who asked him if he had heard about the murder of John Sharpless. "I didn't know nothin' about it before then," Johnson said.

Mollie Stevens was called to the stand next, and her disdain was evident from the moment she entered the room. She countered the claim that she ever officially wed Johnson and in fact testified that after five years of keeping his house, Johnson left her—presumably for Carrie Lane, with whom he'd been found at the time of his arrest.

"Then you don't feel extremely kindly toward the defendant, do you?" asked Magistrate Smith.

"No indeed, I do not," Stevens spat back. "He promised to marry me an' then he left me."

Sensing the magistrate's reservations about Stevens's motives for coming forward, the prosecuting attorney interjected, "This is a competent witness who has never been married to the defendant and is not now living with him and has no relations with him that the law recognizes. If there is any malice, it should be brought up at trial and not at this hearing."

Magistrate Smith allowed the examination to continue.

Stevens told of how she and Johnson had once lived near John Lindsay. Johnson in fact had worked for the farmer but was let go after he stole several of Lindsay's hogs. She said that the night after the murder, she was at the Philadelphia home of Charles Stevens, "keeping house," when Johnson came in and told them he had walked there from Chester.

"What *exactly* did he say?" Magistrate Smith demanded.

Stevens, losing a bit of her bravado in the face of Smith's direct questioning, replied that Johnson said "he had walked a good bit up Darby Road"—a road leading from Delaware County to southwestern Philadelphia, running several miles in total length. He spoke about the fire at Lindsay's barn and said that it was between seven and eight o'clock that night and that it lit up the woods for a good ways all around. "I made a hot fire, and he sat by it all night. He said he was very tired and had been walking a great deal," she said. It was later that night, Stevens testified, that she saw Johnson at Carrie

Lane's house, and it was there that he admitted to setting the barn on fire in revenge for Lindsay's firing him.

Court spectators were fascinated and speculated among themselves. If Johnson spent the evening sitting in front of Mollie's fire, when did he leave for Carrie's house? And why would his "wife" go to his girlfriend's house? The audience watched the trial as if it were one of those novels the newspapers published one chapter at a time, each ending with a cliffhanger sure to make you buy the next issue.

The magistrate gave Johnson the opportunity to respond to Stevens. He flatly denied burning Lindsay's barn, although he admitted to visiting Mollie.

Charles Stevens testified next, although he added little to the proceedings. He said he knew nothing of Samuel Johnson except that he had stayed overnight and that Johnson had spoken of husking corn for a farmer on Darby Road. Likewise, Carrie Lane's testimony was valueless. She denied even a previous acquaintance with Johnson and strongly asserted that she knew nothing about the Sharpless murder.

A police officer who had aided in Johnson's arrest exhibited two coats and two handkerchiefs—all of which he said Johnson admitted to owning. Johnson had no questions for the witness, nor did he provide any explanation to the magistrate.

After this meager testimony concluded, the prosecutor assured the magistrate that, while he had corroborating witnesses who would take at least two more hours to examine, he was of the opinion that enough evidence had already been presented to try Samuel Johnson for murder.

Magistrate Smith—whose attitude throughout the hearing belied a lack of confidence in the prosecutor's case—ordered that Johnson be taken to the Delaware County jail to be held for trial. Mollie Stevens and Carrie Lane were also to be held in the county jail as witnesses.

As he was led back to his holding cell, Johnson seemed to believe his conviction was a bygone conclusion. "I do not expect to be cleared of this charge of murder," he told a prison officer. "I look for them to hang me."

WHILE PHILADELPHIA POLICE made plans to transport Johnson to the jail in Media, Delaware County authorities expressed grave doubts that this was their man. They were hard-pressed to believe the testimony of Mollie Stevens; not only did she harbor ill will toward Johnson, but she was also obviously interested in the reward money. And Susan Sharpless had now reported a new recollection: the clothes of the man who'd entered her home were completely dry and "rather spruce." Would this be true of a man who walked from Philadelphia to her farm in a driving storm? Jane now remembered that the man at the door wore a gossamer jacket and had no handkerchief around his neck. Therefore, any identifications made based on a coarse wool coat and white neckcloth would be questionable.

Never one to take a backseat, Chief Williamson told reporters he had fully investigated Samuel Johnson before arresting John Carpenter and determined he was not a suspect. When, why or how this investigation proceeded, Williamson did not say, so his claims probably served more to chide Philadelphia police for coming late to the game rather than assure the public of his thoroughness.

At three o'clock on the afternoon of December 23, Johnson was led from the Third District station house and transported by police patrol wagon to the Broad Street train station. If he noticed the fuss he created among the many spectators along the way, he did not let on. Instead, he spent the train ride in silence, only speaking when Lieutenant Roche or Special Officer Alexander asked him questions.

Samuel Johnson would remain in the Media jail until March 2, 1886, when the Delaware County Court of Quarter Sessions, which tried criminal cases, would next be called to order.

CHAPTER 7
The Trial

Workmen laid the cornerstone of the courthouse at Media in 1849, the year of Samuel Johnson's birth. The original building was a narrow, deep, two-story structure topped by a very tall clock tower and weather vane. By the 1870s, substantial wings flanked either side of the

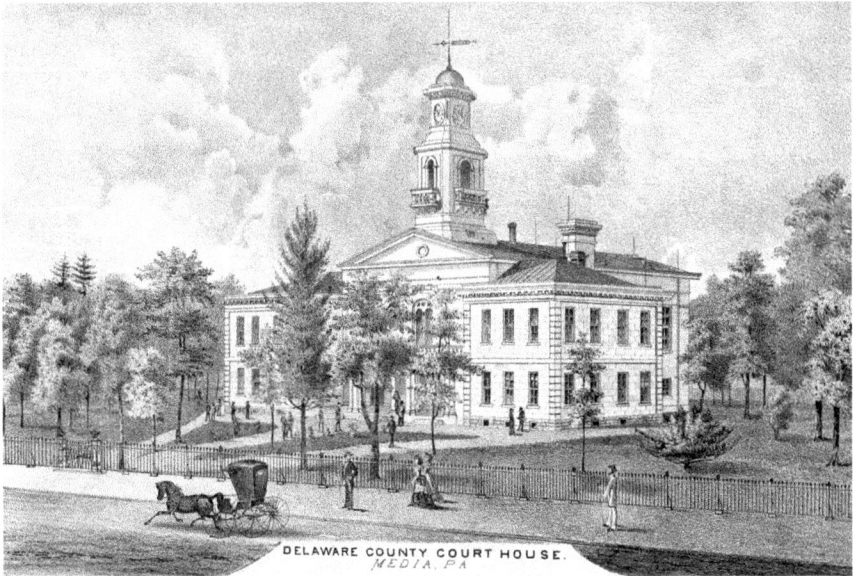

The Delaware County Courthouse in Media very much as it looked at the time of Samuel Johnson's trial. *Image from* Combination Atlas Map of Delaware County.

Receipt for reimbursement of the expenses of Philadelphia special officer Thomas Alexander, who, along with Lieutenant Roche, transported witnesses to Samuel Johnson's trial. *Image created by author from Delaware County court records.*

white building, this extra space necessary to accommodate the business of the multiple counties it served. In 1874, Delaware County became its own separate judicial district, and John M. Broomall, appointed by Governor Hartranft, became the first judge exclusive to the county. Broomall served only one term before losing his bid for reelection to Thomas J. Clayton, who now presided over the Johnson case.

March 2, 1886, was a cold day in southeastern Pennsylvania, with temperatures barely surpassing twenty degrees. This did not deter the crowd's early arrival at the Delaware County Courthouse. Hundreds of spectators sought to claim choice perches from which to watch one of the most notorious trials in county history. No seat was empty, and those who came too late to sit were just as happy standing in the aisles.

While witness Alexander Pritchett was transported from Philadelphia by Lieutenant Roche and S.O. Alexander, Mollie Stevens and Carrie Lane (held in jail while waiting to testify) made the much shorter walk from the Media jail to the nearby courthouse. Other witnesses waited nervously, summonses in hand.

The first order of business was to select a grand jury that would determine if evidence sufficed to try Samuel Johnson on the charges of murder, arson and burglary. A dozen of these potential jurors begged Judge Clayton for release, complaining that the prolonged service required of a grand juror would sorely impact their businesses. "I can consider no business excuses for this term," Clayton tersely replied. Only a handful of the members of the grand jury pool were subsequently dismissed for reasons of their own sickness or the illness of family members.

The impaneled grand jury convened at two o'clock to a packed house of spectators, reporters, witnesses, prospective jurors, lawyers and court personnel. Johnson was represented at these

Judge Thomas Jefferson Clayton, an important cog in Delaware County's nineteenth-century Republican Party machine and the arbiter of much of Samuel Johnson's fate. *Image from* Rambles and Reflections.

proceedings by not one but two lawyers: John B. Robinson and James P. Cummins, one of the attorneys who had represented previous suspect John Carpenter. Only seven of several dozen witnesses testified before the grand jury determined sufficient evidence had been presented to return an indictment. The process took only an hour. Samuel Johnson was not in the courtroom during these proceedings but was brought in immediately after.

Unlike Moyamensing Prison, the jail at Media was small and—as originally constructed—quite easily escaped. Later improvements corrected the problem of the jail's porosity, although it neither aspired to nor achieved the levels of austerity and punishment delivered by Moyamensing or the state prisons. It apparently fed inmates better as well, for on the day Johnson appeared in court both reporters and witnesses noted that he was far plumper than when he'd first arrived. He also now had a new wardrobe. Thanks to his attorneys, Johnson, for very likely the first time in his life, wore a woolen broadcloth suit with a pristine white shirt underneath. Johnson's round face sported a beard, mustache and thick whiskers.

As Johnson entered the courtroom, the crowd swept toward him in that peculiar, synchronized manner that crowds do. The unlucky few not anticipating the surge were knocked down. Johnson was visibly shaken by the wave of bodies coming at him but safely reached his seat. His trial for the murder of John Sharpless had begun.

SAMUEL JOHNSON WAS NOT a fortunate man. Uneducated and born into poverty, his life sharply contrasted with those of the men on either side of him. Johnson's lead attorney, John B. Robinson, was born into a family of legislators, lawyers and military men. He enlisted to serve in the Civil War, but the family already had two sons fighting, so Robinson's grandfather used his influence to have John released from service. As a consolation, Robinson was appointed to the United States Naval Academy at Annapolis. After eleven years of service, he returned to Pennsylvania to study law but made an unplanned foray into publishing, eventually enjoying brief ownership of both the *Delaware County Gazette* and the *Media Ledger*. Robinson was elected state legislator from Delaware County in 1884 and served in that capacity throughout Johnson's trial. His co-counsel, James S. Cummins, was the younger of the two yet had been admitted to the Delaware County Bar six months before Robinson. Their opponent, district attorney Jesse M. Baker, was admitted within days of Cummins.

Like Robinson, Judge Thomas Jefferson Clayton—a seminal force in Delaware County's nineteenth-century Republican political machine—was born to means. He was the oldest of four brothers, all of whom pursued political careers. Powell Clayton was elected governor of Arkansas and then U.S. senator before finally being appointed U.S. minister to Mexico. Younger brother John, also involved in Arkansas politics, was assassinated while running for the U.S. House of Representatives. The killer was never found, and that election has been described as one of the most corrupt in the state's history.

At Judge Clayton's death in 1900, he was earning more than $4,000 per year, nearly ten times the wages of the average American of that day. Over his career, Clayton faced a variety of accusations, including fraudulent election practices and the use of liquor licenses to leverage political support. The most common accusation against the judge was that he decided cases from a personal rather than legal perspective. When delivering a jury charge, Clayton's instructions could appear purposely

Attorney John B. Robinson served as Samuel Johnson's defense counsel from the time of his trial in Delaware County to the conclusion of his appeals process. *Image from* A History of Delaware County and Its People.

contradictory: he would freely express his opinion about the defendant's guilt or innocence yet in the next sentence tell the jurors they should make up their own minds. In light of Clayton's reputation, it is likely that some of the jurymen hearing his cases thought twice about disappointing the powerful judge.

If Clayton might become Johnson's pain, close Sharpless friend John M. Broomall was his tonic. Like Clayton, Broomall came from wealth, but he both attended and taught at Quaker schools, an experience that influenced the remainder of his life.

Broomall won election to the Pennsylvania House of Representatives prior to entering Pennsylvania's Civil War militia as captain of the Twenty-ninth Regiment's Company C. As a member of the U.S. House of Representatives, Broomall served during the final two years of Lincoln's first term. He assumed prominent roles in the passage of the Thirteenth Amendment (which abolished slavery and indentured servitude), Reconstruction legislation and efforts to win the vote for women. Upon returning to Media, Broomall ran for judge and won handily. He publicly opposed capital punishment, saying that no man should be legally executed in Delaware County.

The run-ins between Broomall and Clayton were stuff of Delaware County courtroom legend, and indeed this enmity would bind the two men for the rest of their lives. Broomall's reelection loss to Clayton surely fanned the flames of bitterness, but the two were simply very different men. Broomall returned to the courtroom as an ardent defense lawyer and during one trial became so enraged with Judge Clayton's questioning of his witness that he threatened to walk out mid-testimony. Only Clayton's promise of contempt charges convinced Broomall to return to his seat. While Broomall had no direct hand in the Johnson trial, there is little doubt of his influence on the Sharpless family as a whole and Widow Sharpless in particular.

Whether he understood it or not, the fate of penniless, illiterate, black Samuel Johnson rested in the hands of wealthy, well-bred white men who had far more in common with the victim than they did with the defendant.

Court clerk Elwood Wilson read the charge: murder with force and arms upon the body of John Sharpless. "How do you plead?" Wilson asked the defendant, who seemed uncertain if he should answer.

Robinson prodded Johnson, who finally replied, "Not guilty."

"You *are* guilty," District Attorney Baker shouted, "and the commonwealth is prepared to prove it!"

Johnson's attorneys made no objection or response, and jury selection began. Judge Clayton called for the jury pool, thirty-nine men who, one by one, answered questions. Prospective juror Mark Cummings shared his opinion that Johnson was guilty. He was thanked and told to step aside. The only black man in the pool, Jordan Cavner, was similarly dismissed after telling Judge Clayton that he would need to see a man actually kill someone before he could be convinced of his guilt. Eventually, twelve men good and true were selected, and they included some of Delaware County's best-known citizens. Several of the men were Civil War veterans. Jury foreman John Y. Worrall had served under Captain John M. Broomall.

District Attorney Baker opened the trial just before five o'clock. As if the weight of the job at hand weren't self-evident, he told jurors that they were about to try the most important case in Delaware County history. Slowly and confidently, he reviewed the facts of the murder. At the conclusion of his remarks, Baker produced a heavy iron poker he proclaimed to be the murder weapon—although no such weapon was ever reported found. Again, there were no objections from Johnson's attorneys.

Baker spoke freely of Johnson's previous crimes, his time in Moyamensing Prison and his friendship with Alexander Pritchett. He recounted Johnson's alleged confessions to Pritchett and Mollie Stevens. After forcefully delivering these opening remarks, Judge Clayton adjourned the court until nine o'clock the next morning. Whether by shrewd lawyering or sheer luck, Baker's were the last words the spectators heard before retiring for the evening. As for the jury, this might not have been the case.

In a turn of events unimaginable under the modern legal system, Judge Clayton and the jury were sequestrated together, the county commissioner providing sleeping cots. What, if any, conversation about Samuel Johnson passed between the judge and jury can only be speculated.

THE SECOND DAY of trial opened with a series of witnesses whose function it was to lay the groundwork for the prosecution's case. Joseph and William Mickel both testified to finding the body of John Sharpless and seeing the subsequent fire at the nearby Lindsay barn. Both men described the proximity of John's head to the horse in the first stable. Both agreed the horses were calm and undisturbed when they arrived.

A civil engineer presented a drawing of the Sharpless house and surrounds. The prison warden who had provided Johnson with a coat and pants upon his release from Moyamensing told jurors Johnson now looked different—larger and healthier. Lewis Morris Lewis testified about the robbery at his home and identified the long, black coat found in Johnson's home as being similar to the one taken from him. And Charlie

Stevens swore that Johnson had shown up the morning after the murder telling Mollie about the fire at the Lindsay barn, contradicting his own arraignment testimony.

In a rare move of defiance, Defense Attorney Robinson shouted, "Objection!" when the prosecution called Mollie Stevens to the stand. "She cannot testify. A wife cannot testify against her husband."

Although it is now well known that a spouse cannot be compelled to testify against a husband or wife, at the time of the Sharpless trial there existed an even broader concept of law known as inter-spousal witness immunity. This common law principle prohibited spouses from providing *any* testimony—for or against each other—for fear that what was said might, in the future, affect the marriage or cause a divorce. *How* Johnson's attorneys convinced Clayton they were married is unknown, for at the arraignment it was argued they were not. But since it was established that they were, legally Mollie could not be called as a witness.

To Robinson's objection, therefore, Judge Clayton correctly agreed, and—notwithstanding the obvious disappointment of the jury and spectators—Johnson's wife was barred from taking the stand.

As he had done just hours before in front of the grand jury, Alexander Pritchett again testified to Johnson's confession, by now including details

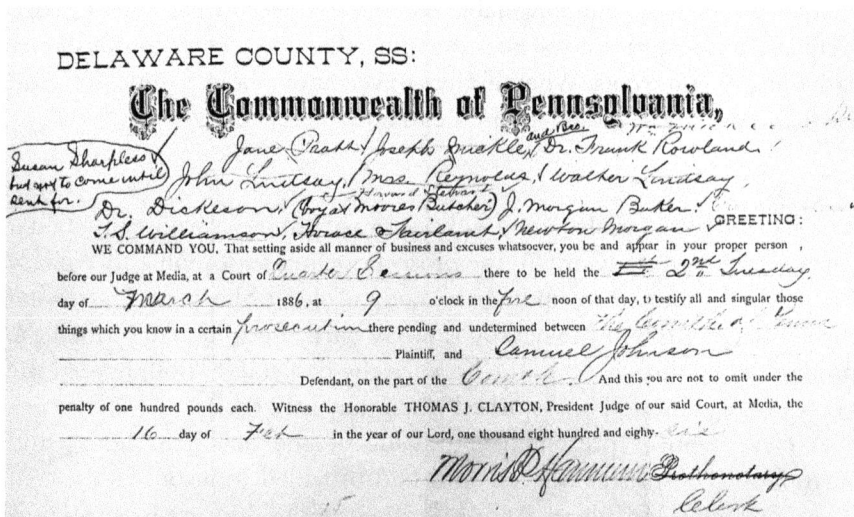

March 1886 summonses of witnesses to testify in the Samuel Johnson trial. A circled note instructs that Susan Sharpless need only arrive at court when sent for. *Image created by author from Delaware County court records.*

such as his recollection about Johnson's fury at finding only six dollars in the Quaker's pockets.

After several more doses of what they had already read in the newspapers, the jurors were about to hear a new voice—the person whose story no one had yet fully learned. It was time for Susan H. Sharpless to take the stand.

Out of deference to the widow and her weakened physical state, the summons included a handwritten notation instructing that Susan should only come to court when sent for. The soft sound of her light, shuffling footsteps was deafening in the dead silence that had fallen over the audience. She was pale. Her gait was excruciatingly slow. She finally reached the witness box where the court clerk waited.

As a Quaker, Susan would not take the oath sworn to by other witnesses. They based this aversion on the teachings of Jesus, who, in his Sermon on the Mount, instructed his followers about oaths by admonishing them to not swear at all. For Quakers, this meant both profane as well as judicial swearing. Since Friends believed in speaking honestly at all times, the swearing of an oath somehow implied a double standard—one set of truths in their everyday lives and another in the courtroom. The alternative was an affirmation that, although carrying the same legal weight, allowed Quakers to maintain their principles.

Every ear strained to hear Susan's affirmation except perhaps Samuel Johnson's. He was seated just feet away from the witnesses. Susan was seeing him for the first time. Unlike Carpenter and Brown, Johnson was never brought to her home for identification. Her health had so deteriorated after the murder that her doctor forbade it.

District Attorney Baker asked Susan to describe the events of the evening of November 22, 1885. Everyone—from judge to jury to spectators—leaned forward to hear her quiet account. Every word Susan uttered was carefully weighed. She recalled with great precision how someone had knocked on her door about eight thirty that night asking for a piece of rope to mend a broken wagon. She described her husband's response and his immediate decision to leave the house with the stranger. Susan spoke of Jane's decision to search for John when he didn't return after half an hour.

Almost immediately after Jane left, "a tall colored man entered the sitting room where I was engaged in writing," Susan testified. "He came in slowly, took two or three steps into the room and then stopped and spoke something. I could not distinguish the words but accepted it as a salutation. He came nearer, and I went nearer to him. Then he stood perfectly still, and I asked him what he wanted. He answered, 'I want a little money.' I said, 'We are not in the habit of keeping money in the house, and I cannot give thee any.' He then said, with much emphasis, 'But I want some.' I passed by him, walking around the table. I went around three times without stopping."

Susan told the jury that the stranger next asked if there was a young girl in the house. Thinking he had mistaken the servant girl for her daughter, Susan explained, "Thee cannot see her. She is not our child, and thee cannot see her." She also testified that Lydia Reynolds offered to call the black man who worked on the Sharpless farm if he preferred to speak to him, but by then the stranger had turned to leave.

"He went slowly, stopped in the doorway, seemed to hesitate whether to go or not. Then he took a step or two out in the hallway. At this point, I was so close to him that I could put my hands on him. After he went out, I fastened the door."

Asked to describe the man, Susan said, "His clothing was dark. He wore a soft hat and white handkerchief around his throat, apparently fastened behind. He had no overcoat. He wore a dress coat of pretty good length."

District Attorney Baker momentarily ceased questioning the witness to retrieve the coat Johnson was alleged to have left behind at the home of Lewis Morris Lewis. He handed it to Susan, who examined it cautiously.

"Is this the coat?" he asked.

"It is similar," Susan said.

With the flourish of a magician, Baker stripped off his own jacket and slipped on the coat held in evidence. "Is this the coat?" he repeated.

Susan once more responded that it was similar.

"Can you describe the man who entered your home that night?" Baker asked.

After a short pause, Susan said, "The man had a large nose, lips that stood out, and he had two front teeth that I took particular notice of—they seemed to be quite prominent. I have no recollection of him covering them with his lips while I saw them."

"How does the prisoner compare in height in weight?" asked Baker, who now—without asking permission of the judge and without objection from Clayton or the defense—asked Samuel Johnson to come stand before Susan Sharpless.

Every neck in the courtroom craned to see the defendant, and every listener concentrated on Susan's quiet response.

"Keep in mind," cautioned Baker, "that the whiskers, beard and mustache worn by the prisoner have grown since his incarceration with the exception of a little knotty mustache."

Susan studied Johnson. "I don't think the man was as tall as this man," she said. "But his weight corresponds." This was an interesting comment considering that a previous witness had pointed out that Johnson's weight had only been gained while awaiting trial in the Media jail. Neither of Johnson's attorneys pointed this out to the jury, and Baker certainly knew better than to mention it.

"Please push up your upper lip," he commanded Johnson, who did so without hesitation. "Repeat these phrases," he told Johnson, who, as directed, said, "I want money" and "I want some."

"Is there a similarity in the voices?" Baker asked.

"I believe there is," Susan replied, "but the teeth do not stand out as much as the other man. They do not show as plainly when he talks."

When the time finally came for cross-examination, Robinson asked Susan the race of the man who had entered her home the night of the murder. "He was not fully black," she said, "but neither was he mulatto."

In one final round of questioning, Baker asked the widow how Johnson's color compared to the stranger's. "Very much that color," she said.

Turning to the jury, Baker asked one final question: "Can you identify the defendant as the man who was in your house that night?"

Judge Clayton—as did all in attendance—leaned closer to hear her response.

"I think I am not able to do it," Susan said.

DAY THREE OF THE TRIAL was again dominated by the prosecution. Dr. Rowland, who conducted the postmortem, testified that John Sharpless's wounds could not have been inflicted by the kick of a horse. William Hahn, a young newspaper seller in Philadelphia, told jurors that on the morning after the murder, a tall, thin black man asked for a newspaper containing the account of a fire and murder near Chester. The boy told him there was no such paper. Johnson was again ordered to stand so the paperboy could get a full look at him. After careful inspection, the boy responded that he looked similar to the man who had approached the newsstand. What Johnson's lawyers did not ask the witness, however, was why a man who couldn't read would want a newspaper.

The most interesting of the day's witnesses was John Norris, city editor for the *Philadelphia Record*. This daily newspaper had debuted in May 1870 under the slightly longer title *Philadelphia Public Record*. Commissions were paid to a small army of canvassers to cultivate the sale of subscriptions, and this strategy swiftly swelled the paper's circulation to more than 100,000 readers. Unfortunately, it turned out that the canvassers' exuberance surpassed their honesty, and many of the new "subscribers" proved to be fictitious. Readership plunged, and the paper was sold. The new owner determined to make it cheaper to buy (the issue price fell from two cents to one) and more interesting to read. By 1880, the *Record* was known for breaking scandals, including corruption in the coroner's office and the illegal sale of human cadavers. Determined to report news first, pneumatic tubes were installed to whisk dispatches from the telegrapher's office to the editor's desk in twenty-eight seconds. The paper thrived under an editorial policy of quick deadlines and titillating headlines. No story attracted more readers than that of the murder by a black man of Quaker John Sharpless in his own barn while his sickly wife waited unaware inside their warm, well-appointed home.

The legal, investigative and journalistic standards of 1885 were vastly different from those of today. Members of the police force were free to accept remuneration from sources outside of their employ, and newspapers regularly paid them for information. During the Sharpless investigation, both Lieutenant Roche and Special Officer Alexander were paid by the *Philadelphia Record* to assist reporter John J. Curley in investigating the case. No one, including Samuel Johnson's attorneys, pointed out the illicit temptation inherent in this arrangement—one surely encouraged by the additional $3,000 in reward money also at stake.

John Norris did not just cover the story. He became a witness for the prosecution. Apparently, Johnson's lawyers neglected to advise their client against speaking about the case, for Norris interviewed him on four separate occasions without the presence of counsel. Norris revealed alleged contradictions uncovered during these interviews in his trial testimony. The defense did little to challenge his accounts, nor did it protest the admission of Norris's account of walking the same path he proposed Johnson took on the night of the murder. Norris authoritatively assured the jury that he had proven the time line the defense offered could not possibly be accurate. Both Lieutenant Roche and Reporter Curley were called to the stand to substantiate Norris's testimony.

A day that began with whispers of a possible surprise witness to be introduced by Johnson's attorneys ended with Robinson and Cummins utilizing just thirty minutes for their tepid defense. No one was called to explain exactly where Samuel Johnson was at the time of John Sharpless's killing. In fact, it was as if his lawyers hoped to avoid the topic altogether—not surprising since no solid alibi could be offered. Efforts were made to impeach the testimony of Alexander Pritchett. One witness claimed to have been with Johnson during the time Pritchett and he were supposedly drinking together. Another said he saw Johnson and his wife walking along the street at ten o'clock on Monday morning, although this served no significant purpose other than to suggest such behavior would be unlikely if Johnson had killed a man just hours before.

The most intriguing defense witness was John Lindsay, owner of the burned barn. He told jurors that he knew Samuel Johnson and that Johnson—up until being caught stealing a sow—had worked for him. Lindsay also said Johnson did handyman jobs for John Sharpless. Had it been Johnson who came to the door that Sunday night, surely Sharpless would have recognized him, Lindsay testified. And there would have been no question as to his race. But this information had little impact on the audience, nor did the jury seem particularly impressed. The defense then rested, although some felt it was never that lively to begin with.

Judge Clayton invited both sides to offer closing arguments. Robinson spoke first. For more than three hours—far longer than he'd spent questioning witnesses—he offered reasons for the jury to find reasonable doubt in the prosecution's case. Didn't John Sharpless tell his sister-in-law that the man at the door was white? And Susan Sharpless never positively identified Samuel Johnson. Wouldn't she know if Samuel Johnson was the stranger who stood within arm's distance of her the night of the murder? And what of the *Philadelphia Record*? The newspaper had so much as told its readers that Samuel Johnson was the killer of John Sharpless, prejudicing the public toward his guilt. John J. Curley's "investigation" was nothing more than an opportunity to remind people that they had beaten the competition to reporting his capture. And in between each point, Robinson again and again reminded the jury that John Sharpless himself had believed the man at his door to be white. That alone should create sufficient doubt in the minds of twelve men in the jury box, Robinson said.

It was nine o'clock by the time District Attorney Baker closed the trial with his own final arguments. He told jurors that, rather than relying on the victim's description of the man at the door, they should instead recall the testimony of Jane Pratt. She, after all, also spoke to the caller. She believed him to be black. Unlike Robinson, or perhaps precisely because of his lengthy final argument, Baker was brief. He was confident the commonwealth had proven its case. He expected the jury to be confident as well. Once again, his would be the final words addressed to the jury before court adjourned.

As it did every morning, the bell in the courthouse cupola sounded nine o'clock, but the people of Delaware County needed no reminder of the time. Testimony in the Johnson trial was finished. It was now Judge Clayton's job to turn the case over to the jury. Several hundred people waited in high anticipation to hear his instructions.

Clayton's charge to the jury began immediately after the bell and went on for ninety minutes. Like the trial itself, it was a lopsided performance. For more than an hour, Clayton discussed the prosecution's case. Only the last several minutes of his jury charge were devoted to the defense. He began with those well-worn words from courtrooms past: "Gentlemen of the jury." Every eye and ear turned toward Clayton—except for Samuel Johnson's. Instead, he stared fixedly at an empty corner.

"As the learned district attorney has said," Clayton remarked, "we are engaged in the performance of a disagreeable duty. We must perform it, however, conscientiously and to the best of our ability."

Clayton continued on in his practiced, solemn and direct style. "Samuel Johnson is charged with having willfully murdered John Sharpless, a very reputable citizen of this county. The question for you is to decide whether he is guilty or not guilty of that crime."

Whether District Attorney Baker was "learned" or John Sharpless was "reputable" were probably conclusions Clayton should have allowed the jury to draw. Instead, he went on to offer details that had never been drawn from the witnesses. Contradicting Dr. Rowland, Clayton said, "There is a possibility, perhaps, that John Sharpless was not murdered. There is a possibility he may have fallen in a fit, that he may have struck his head and that the horse may have trod upon him, or kicked him, while down. But it will not do for the jury to engage in these speculative doubts. The law does not recognize them. You are to decide according to the weight of the evidence."

The courtroom remained rapt as Clayton recounted briefly the events of the night of November 22, 1885: "It seems to me, therefore, you may find that John Sharpless was murdered. Then comes the second question: by whom was he murdered?"

Clayton's head swept from one side of the jury box to the other, briefly making eye contact with each man before moving on. "The commonwealth says 'by the prisoner.' The defendant denies it. If you find on the first question that he was murdered, you have got over one difficulty; but the great one will be 'by whom was the deed committed?' You have heard the evidence of the commonwealth, and it seems to point to this defendant as the man who committed the crime. It will be for you to say if the evidence warrants a conviction. I say the evidence seems to point to this defendant as the murderer. It undoubtedly does."

Clayton paused, perhaps an automatic response when anticipating an objection from the defense attorney. None came. He continued, now seemingly playing down his own convictions. "I do not intend, if I can avoid it, to give you the slightest intimation of my own judgment," he assured the jury. "But if you shall come to the conclusion that this man is the murderer, then your next great question will be: what is the degree?"

Clayton now embarked on a lengthy diatribe meant to clarify the difference between first- and second-degree murder. If Sharpless was struck and killed in an attempt to rob him, Clayton explained, the finding must be murder in the first degree. "If, however, you find that he had any other project than that of arson, robbery, burglary or rape and only intended to do great bodily harm to John Sharpless when he struck him, then he is guilty of murder in the second degree."

The mention of "rape" in Clayton's charge most surely would have been surprising. There had been no testimony or evidence suggesting such an act was contemplated let alone attempted. Yet both Robinson and Cummins sat quiet and undisturbed, waiting for the judge's instructions to end. But Clayton went on for an hour longer.

Witness by witness, Clayton relayed to the jury what he found to be the most salient parts of the trial. Again they heard about Alexander Pritchett, to whom "your closest attention ought to be directed." The judge was fully endorsing Pritchett, the fellow convict with whom Johnson served time in Moyamensing Prison. The same Pritchett whose most recent testimony suddenly included a description of Johnson's great temper and his complaint that he had found only six dollars in the dead man's pockets (even though the clothing of John Sharpless was described by other witness as "undisturbed" and his wife reported nothing stolen). Clayton gave an almost line-by-line replay of Pritchett's version of events, ending with an assurance that the jury could believe this man regardless of his criminal history—or his interest in a large reward.

"The mere fact that he has been convicted of assault and battery is not sufficient to throw discredit upon him as a witness. If a witness is convicted of a felony it sometimes is sufficient, but even the mere fact that he is now under arrest for robbery is not in itself sufficient to discredit him."

If they caught it, Clayton's brief mention of Pritchett's current incarceration seemed to have little effect on the jury.

In a backhanded show of sympathy, Clayton advised the jury to give the defendant credit for his inability to produce witnesses in his defense. "You will remember that he has been in jail and that he is poor and friendless. If the prisoner had means, he could perhaps have secured some witnesses. I only call your attention to the fact that it has not been done."

Clayton next delivered his views on the testimony of Susan Sharpless—although he described her as only the "next most important" witness after criminal Alexander Pritchett. In a remarkable turn of fairness, Clayton declared that Susan's testimony cast more doubt on the commonwealth's case than that of any other witness. And yet he spent only several minutes describing it to the jury. "Unless [Johnson] disguised himself," Clayton said, "the subject does not comport with Mrs. Sharpless's description."

Clayton offered the same theory of a possible disguise when revisiting the testimony of John Lindsay. "He tells you his barn was burned that night. He also tells you he knew the defendant and that he believes John Sharpless knew him as well. Unless he disguised himself, the presumption is that John Sharpless would know Samuel Johnson."

On a number of occasions, Clayton told the jury that witnesses had "identified" the coat Johnson wore when in fact they had testified only that it was "similar" in appearance to that which was being exhibited. He recounted the testimony offered by the newsboy, who said he had been asked by a black man for a newspaper containing an account of a barn fire and murder yet neglected to mention that Johnson could not read. Perhaps Clayton's most interesting comments were the words of praise heaped on John Norris and Special Officer Alexander. Norris, Clayton emphatically offered, "seems to have exercised more than ordinary energy in endeavoring to ferret out this murder. He is to be commended for that, not condemned." As to the $125 paid to Special Officer Alexander, "There was nothing wrong with that. It was given to cover incidental expenses incurred in working up the case."

Clayton spent less than five minutes discussing the case presented by the defense. "The defendant alleges mistaken identity. He says that Pritchett is anxious to get him out of the way in order to get the reward. He says his wife is anxious to get rid of him that she may live with another man. He also relies upon the failure of Mrs. Sharpless to identify him." Of the few witnesses the defense did call to the stand, Clayton suggested, "Their testimony corroborates one side about as much as the other."

Finally, Clayton sent the jury to deliberate. "We have done our part, and you must now do yours. Do it conscientiously, and the court will be satisfied with your verdict."

CHAPTER 8
The Verdict

Judge Thomas Jefferson Clayton instructed court officers to ring the courthouse bell when the jury reached a verdict. He expected his jury charge would enable a quick decision. But by eight o'clock on the evening of March 5, 1886, no bell had yet sounded. Clayton ordered that the courtroom lights be turned off and told the staff and spectators to go home.

What might have been black and white to Clayton was far more shadowy to the jury, whose first act was to take a vote to see where things stood. All agreed that Johnson was guilty. Nine jury members voted for first-degree murder, with the remainder voting second degree. Three men prevented the jury from reaching unanimous agreement. One man, foreman John Y. Worrall, felt strongly enough to put up a prolonged fight.

Even when the balance increased to ten against two, Worrall stubbornly clung to his conviction that Johnson had not acted with an intent to kill. He could not convict the man of first-degree murder, he told fellow jurymen, if Johnson did not mean for John Sharpless to die.

Hours into deliberations and well into the early morning hours the jury again polled itself. The count was eleven to one in favor of first-degree murder. Worrall was the lone holdout for conviction in the second degree.

Seeking more to end the trial than acquiesce to fellow jurors, after sixteen hours of deliberations Worrall voted with the majority. They would wait until sunrise to inform Judge Clayton that a verdict had been reached.

As it was every morning, court was called to order at nine o'clock to the second. The judge, rigid and upright in his chair, waited for the jury's appearance. Samuel Johnson sat between attorneys John B. Robinson and James S. Cummins. His expression, as it had been through most of the trial, was blank—almost disinterested.

The jury entered the courtroom led by a tipstaff carrying a hickory pole. In decades past, this court employee would have used the pole to prod jurors nodding off during testimony. It was a function highly unnecessary during the trial of Samuel Johnson.

As had come to be expected, the gallery held several hundred people anxious to hear Johnson's fate. The audience had followed this drama from the beginning; they weren't going to miss the ending. All eyes fell on the court clerk.

"Prisoner, stand up," he said to Johnson.

Johnson rose without hesitation. He looked steadily at the jurors, probably because his lawyers had instructed him to do so.

"Prisoner, look upon the jury," the clerk ordered. "Jurors, look upon the prisoner. How say you in the case of the *Commonwealth of Pennsylvania v. Samuel Johnson*. Do you find him guilty in the manner and form he stands indicted or not guilty?"

Looking tired yet sounding resolute, foreman Worrall answered, "Guilty as indicted."

An excited murmur ran through the crowd then instantly ceased of its own accord.

"If guilty," asked the clerk, "in what degree?"

"In the first degree," said Worrall.

The crowd, finally free to release its nervous tension, erupted in babble. District Attorney Baker felt for the armrests as he slowly lowered himself into his chair. Disbelief flashed across his face, for even he knew the weakness of his case.

Robinson and Cummins leaned forward to consult each other, speaking around their client.

A perceptible shiver ran through Samuel Johnson, who for the first time seemed to understand that he would never again see life through anything but prison glass.

"I request the jury be polled," Robinson said to Judge Clayton. One by one, the jurors were asked to state their verdict. One by one, they said, "Guilty of murder in the first degree." Johnson slumped backward in his seat.

Judge Clayton thanked the jurors for their service and discharged them from the courtroom.

"I motion for a new trial," Robinson said immediately upon their departure.

Clayton paused, studying the attorneys and their client. "You have four days to file your reasons for requesting this new trial," he told Robinson. "I'll hear your arguments the first Monday in April." Turning to Sheriff William T. Mathues, Clayton ordered that the prisoner be returned to his cell in the Media jail, across the street behind the courthouse.

Johnson's attorneys told reporters they were not surprised by the verdict and had, in truth, even expected it. They were convinced their client would be freed at the conclusion of a second trial. "We have very excellent grounds for a new trial," Robinson told reporters, "mainly after-discovered evidence, and I think the court will be inclined to look favorably on the motion. We looked for acquittal until the judge's charge, which left a loophole for second-degree murder, and we then thought the

EXTRA!

SECOND EDITION !

THE VERDICT.

The Jury Finds John-son Guilty as In-dicted.

Murder----First Degree

After Hours of Deliberation the Twelve Men Find That the Prisoner Was the Slay-er of John Sharpless.

A BIG CROWD HEARS THE VERDICT.

This *Chester Evening Times* headline announcing Samuel Johnson's guilty verdict was similar to many around the state and nation.

jury would find that verdict. Johnson, in our opinion, is innocent of this crime, and Mr. Cummins and myself will not cease our efforts to clear him."

Judge Clayton was equally certain that the matter had come to lasting conclusion. "I have very little doubt of the prisoner's guilt," he told the *Philadelphia Record*, "although I thought the jury might render a verdict of guilty in the second degree."

A great stir ensued after it was reported that Clayton told a juror, "If Johnson, poor fellow, is not the man, Pritchett is his murderer." The *Record* was forceful in its assertion that this was a misquote. What Clayton actually said, according to the newspaper, was: "If Johnson, poor fellow, is hanged, and it is afterward shown that he is innocent, Pritchett is his murderer." Clayton himself never denied or corrected either statement.

THE CASE THAT SERVED to captivate the community also served to divide it after the verdict was rendered. Some believed it was the right outcome. Others were shocked that a guilty verdict could be reached on such indecisive and circumstantial evidence. Still others felt that the threat of a death sentence would prompt Johnson to confess—or at the very least give up the names of anyone who might have helped him the night of the murder.

The theory that more than one man was involved in the killing of John Sharpless was quickly gaining ground. Chief Williamson was open about his belief that Alexander Pritchett was that second man. District Attorney Baker, more circumspect in this opinion, said he, too, had a second suspect in mind but would not divulge the race of the man or any other details. The fact that Susan said the man *inside* the home wore a handkerchief around his neck and Jane Pratt reported the man *outside* did not served to fan the flames of speculation even higher. There had to be, most observers agreed, two perpetrators.

Jury foreman John Y. Worrall had hoped to hedge his bets with regards to Johnson's punishment. "I thought it would be better to return a verdict of murder in the second degree," he told the *Chester Times*, "for he then would be sent to jail. Should anything occur to show we were mistaken, he could be released."

On the first Monday in April 1886, John B. Robinson appeared before Judge Clayton. He assured the judge he was working on newly uncovered clues and asked for a postponement of the argument for a new trial. Clayton gave Johnson's attorneys until the first week in May. On the first Monday in May, the attorneys again asked for a postponement. They presented to the judge a statement from George Myers, now serving time in Moyamensing Prison for robbery, describing how a fellow prisoner named English Tom had confessed to the Sharpless murder. Clayton and District Attorney Baker agreed to postpone arguments until October, although Baker had heard this same story previously and considered it unfounded. The October arguments were postponed until December 7, when Judge Thomas J. Clayton finally heard Robinson's justifications for a new trial.

The calmest person in the room appeared to be Samuel Johnson. He chewed happily on tobacco while listening to the proceedings. After brief consideration and a negligible delay, Judge Clayton denied the defense counsel's request and sentenced Johnson to hang. With this sentence, Johnson would earn two distinctions: he would be the first man sentenced to death in Delaware County in nearly half a century and the first man to receive this sentence in the present courthouse.

When asked if he had any comments, Samuel Johnson said only that he understood he had been convicted. With that he was led back to his cell to await his execution.

CHAPTER 9

Appeals and Petitions

Attorney John B. Robinson was convinced that the one area in which an appeal might be granted was Judge Clayton's inaction when Johnson was asked to stand before witnesses and repeat the phrases used by the intruder inside the Sharpless home. This, said Robinson, was self-incrimination and a violation of Johnson's Fifth Amendment rights. Substantially weakening his argument, however, was the fact that Robinson had not objected to this during the trial itself. That failing aside, Robinson took Johnson's case before the Pennsylvania Supreme Court in January 1887. On February 7, 1887, Justice James P. Sterret delivered an opinion affirming the lower court's actions: "The trial appears to have been conducted with due regard to the rights of the prisoner; and we find nothing in the record that would justify a reversal of the judgment. Judgment affirmed, and it is ordered that the record be remitted for the purpose of carrying the sentence into execution."

By 1887, Johnson had already been spared from the gallows three times, but how long could his luck last? How often would he be read the death warrant and forced to await the awful, long walk to the rope only to learn—as if the victim of some cruel joke—that his date of death had been delayed? This unimaginable cycle of terror, resignation and relief was a constant strain that would weaken any man.

In August 1887, Johnson learned he would live until October 6. In October, he learned that the date had been pushed to November. The November date was delayed until December.

Johnson now had but one final legal option: an appeal to the United States Supreme Court. Counsel for the prisoner made application to Justice Joseph P. Bradley seeking a writ of error based on the asserted violation of Johnson's Fifth Amendment rights. If granted, this would secure the new trial Johnson so desperately needed if he were to have any chance of seeing his conviction overturned. Unfortunately, Justice Bradley's view mirrored the decision of the Pennsylvania Supreme Court. In early March 1888, the court of last resort told Johnson's attorneys it would not hear his case. Johnson would, as Judge Clayton originally sentenced, hang on March 15, and he indeed came very close to death. A gallows was constructed and a hangman retained. Johnson's lawyers furiously dashed off appeals to Pennsylvania's Board of Pardons, but they could neither be sent nor delivered. A massive blizzard had settled over the eastern coast of the United States. Railroads were blocked, mail delivery halted and telegraph wires down. All communication with Harrisburg, where the Board of Pardons was located, was lost. The Delaware County sheriff told Johnson his time had come and implored the doomed man to confess. "I am innocent," replied Johnson. "I have nothing to confess." Finally, just hours before Johnson was to hang, messages were exchanged, and word came that a reprieve had been granted.

Although the Board of Pardons was the public body delivering his reprieves, the key man keeping Johnson alive was Governor James Beaver. Like the Sharpless family, Beaver's ancestors had braved the Atlantic to immigrate to America. Rather than arriving from England, however, they traveled from their ancestral home in the German region known as the Palatinate. After graduating from Jefferson College in western Pennsylvania, Beaver returned to Centre County to study law. Answering the Union's call, Beaver enlisted in the Civil War as first lieutenant of the Bellefont Fencibles. He rose through the ranks to become lieutenant colonel, then colonel and finally brevet brigadier general. But Beaver was not content to serve as an officer removed from the field of battle; he was also a brave and relentless warrior who suffered several serious wounds, the worst of which was the loss of his leg at Ream's Station. After the war, he resumed his law career and became a successful businessman. The leadership of Pennsylvania's Republican Party convinced Beaver that the fighting that had scarred him also made him an attractive candidate for political office. He ran for governor and lost, then tried again four

Pennsylvania governor James A. Beaver was sworn into office in 1887. Samuel Johnson's appeals were some of the first orders of business to cross his desk. *Image from* La Vie, *Pennsylvania State University yearbook.*

years later. Beaver was sworn into the office of governor in 1887. Samuel Johnson's reprieves were some of the first orders of business to cross his desk. It seems unlikely that a man who himself had come close to death several times would view the taking of any life—by murder or legal execution—an easy decision with which to live.

WHILE SAMUEL JOHNSON's attorneys worked within the legal system to try to win his release, the Quaker community and other interested parties worked earnestly and steadfastly outside of it. Many Friends expressed the belief that not protesting the death sentence was tantamount to a sin of participation.

A petition was circulated to the clerks of all monthly meetings in the Delaware County region. They and all meeting members were asked to sign it. The simple act of adding their names offered relief to those Quakers whose consciences forbade them to remain silent. It also allowed Friends to share their view with the Christian community at large that capital punishment was both barbarous and inhumane. Even while grieving the brutal murder of one of their own, the petition was an eloquent appeal for Johnson's life:

> *Believing in the sacredness of human life and in the sinfulness of its destruction, whether by legal enactment or otherwise; and further believing that the safety of the community may be better provided for by the imprisonment of its criminals, this meeting unites in petitioning your body for a commutation of the death sentence passed upon Samuel Johnson, now awaiting execution at Media, Delaware County.*
>
> *We are unwilling to remain silent when an eminently proper opportunity is afforded of bearing our testimony against capital punishment and its train of depraving influences, appalling in their nature.*
>
> *We are strengthened in our appeal by the existence of a wide-spread feeling of doubt as to Johnson's guilt of the murder of John Sharpless. His imprisonment may prevent an injustice for which no human effort could atone.*

This petition, and the nearly five thousand signatures of support on it, was just one of the lobbying efforts directed toward the Board of

Pardons. The unshakable belief by so many in Johnson's innocence began to weigh on the board. Even more influential, however, was the mounting evidence suggesting that others might have perpetrated the crime.

CHAPTER 10
Other Suspects

During the original investigation into the murder of John Sharpless, nearly fifty men—most of them black—were arrested or questioned in connection with the crime.

Several jailhouse snitches passed along the supposed confessions of fellow inmates. Most of these were ignored by the police and the defense team except for George Myers, whose statement was useful in obtaining a postponement.

Men seeking notoriety or fulfillment of some other unusual fantasy offered false, self-incriminating confessions. One such individual, John Cokely, arrived at the Lehigh County Prison asking to whom he might confess murdering John Sharpless. He did so, he said, because he could not bear the thought of Samuel Johnson hanging for a crime he did not commit. Cokely, a white man, was in his mid-forties, slightly built and of an unimpressive height. He explained that he was in Chester at the time of the murder because he had taken a job as a boilermaker for one of the shipyards. He could not be located after the crime, he explained, because he was living and traveling between Florida and Virginia.

Cokely was quite calm as he recounted his story and seemed to police in Allentown to be perfectly rational. Based on his sworn confession, he was arrested and charged with murder. His transport to Delaware County was arranged, but soon word arrived that saved the Lehigh County police the trip. It seemed the Delaware County authorities were already well aware of John Cokely; in fact, he had been in their jail at

Media at the time the murder occurred. There was no way he could have killed John Sharpless.

When faced with these facts, Cokely recanted his confession, saying that he only took credit for the crime in hope of receiving free transit to Chester.

In all the chatter about who—other than Samuel Johnson—might have actually slain John Sharpless, one group of men was suggested time and time again: the notorious Fernwood Gang.

For more than a year starting in the summer of 1885, residents of Delaware County were terrorized by a systematic series of well-planned robberies. Brinton Walton was, by all accounts, a respectable member of the community. His friendships and knowledge of who lived where and owned what was the basis of the gang's hit list. "Big Charlie" Wilson, college educated, was both the strategist and an accomplished safecracker. Mat Connor was the fence. Christopher "Dutch Gus" Chopaz did the actual dirty work of breaking into houses and businesses.

Four Philadelphia police officers tailed the gang members for several weeks during the spring of 1886. That March, a shoe store outside the city was robbed, its contents carried off in a wagon. Police followed the wagon to Mat Connor's house, waited until the goods were offloaded and then staged their raid. Wilson, Chopaz, Brinton and Connor were arrested for possession of stolen property and tried in June in the courtroom of Judge Thomas J. Clayton. All four were found guilty and sentenced immediately. Wilson, who pleaded guilty from the start, received eight years in the county jail. Walton, the only one of the men to offer a defense, received three years at Eastern State Penitentiary. Chopaz and Connor were sentenced to eight years in this same institution. The people of Delaware County were relieved yet more than a little suspicious. Could these be the men who had tried to rob the Sharpless family the previous November? Their modus operandi was certainly more in line with the details of the crime. Johnson, the unsuccessful pig snatcher, would be hard pressed to match such plotting and precision.

In July 1887, both the *New York Times* and the *World* confidently reported that yet another murder suspect had been unearthed, a man whose obvious guilt was certain to help overturn Samuel Johnson's wrongful conviction. If you wanted to know who really killed John Sharpless, you needed look no further, the reports claimed, than William T. Colwell, who sat in the Lancaster County jail awaiting trial for arson.

At one time, Colwell owned a barbershop in Media. It was situated on the ground floor of the Broomall law offices. This fact prompted the logical conclusion that Colwell not only knew John Sharpless but also likely had some understanding of his financial means. Adding to this presumption of familiarity was the fact that Colwell's wife worked at Swarthmore College, just a mile and a half from the Sharpless homestead.

Colwell had fallen under suspicion primarily because of the efforts of a Lancaster County police detective named Edward Barnholt. Barnholt was born in Philadelphia and came to Lancaster County after the Civil War. His biggest brush with fame, according to a published biographical sketch, was when he helped "capture John Atzerodt, one of the conspirators in the killing of Abraham Lincoln," at "Fort Dicks." In actuality, John Atzerodt was not a conspirator but rather the police officer brother of George Atzerodt, who *was* involved in the plot and subsequently hanged. Whether Barnholt was unaware of these errors prior to publication or offered these details himself, we do not know.

In 1883, Barnholt was appointed to Lancaster's police force. In 1887, he was promoted to detective. His investigation into Colwell was conducted privately and without, apparently, the knowledge of his superiors. Barnholt supposedly traced Colwell's whereabouts to within a short distance from the scene of the murder. Individuals interviewed assured Barnholt that Colwell possessed a criminal nature and would not hesitate to take a human life if it was to his benefit or self-protection.

Colwell told different acquaintances different stories about where he was at the time of the crime, although several witnesses placed him in West Chester early on the day of the murder. He was accompanied by a young man named William King. Rumor had it that mail found near the murder scene was supposedly addressed to R.H. Zaboy—one of Colwell's aliases.

Most damning, Colwell's appearance and manner of speech coincided perfectly with that described by the Widow Sharpless. His front teeth protruded, and he wore a black coat, a slouch hat and a white handkerchief tied about his neck.

While in jail, Colwell was visited by a reporter from the *World*, who described him as speaking as though he wore ill-fitting dentures. During the interview, Colwell complained that the people of Christiana bore a grudge against him and that some had even accused him of being Sharpless's murderer—surprising since the reporter had not asked about the case.

The *World* story claimed that both John M. Broomall and Chief Williamson were, early on, made aware of Colwell's suspicious behavior and similarity to the man described by Susan Sharpless. Williamson determined, however, that it was best to keep the information quiet since the Samuel Johnson trial was already underway. Whether or not this is true, Colwell was investigated and ruled out as a suspect after the stories appeared in the newspapers.

In the spring of 1888, the Fernwood Gang again caught the interest of investigators. Authorities learned that not only was Brinton Walton near the Sharpless homestead on the night of the murder, but he was also seen standing with others who had gathered in the yard of John Lindsay to watch his barn burn.

Sam Tate, a lesser member of the gang serving time in Moyamensing Prison for counterfeiting, admitted to police that his confederates had some hand in the crime. Tate said that he, too, would have been with the gang on November 22, 1885, had he not been in Jefferson Hospital with a leg injury. The Philadelphia chief of detectives who took Tate's statement was convinced of the veracity of this new information. He told reporters, "I do not think it would be proper to say anything about the information we have obtained as it might defeat the object we are after; however, there has been enough discovered to raise a reasonable doubt in any man's mind [about Johnson's guilt]."

Other witnesses had also come forward—respectable men outside of the prison system. One man identified Wilson, Chopaz and Walton from photographs as the three men he'd seen driving a wagon away from the Sharpless farm the night of the murder. Another witness remembered Wilson purchasing a black mask at a shop in Philadelphia just prior to the crime. A revolver found on the road skirting the Sharpless farm was identified as one Wilson stole from the home of Richard Seybold, a farmer whose land bordered the murdered Quaker's.

Johnson's attorneys were chomping at the bit to get the case before Judge Clayton, but there was a problem: his honor was on one of his many visits to Europe. Clayton was, for his day, an incredibly well-traveled man and in fact wrote a book about his adventures verbosely entitled *Rambles and Reflections: Europe from Biscay to the Black Sea and from Aetna to the North Cape with Glimpses at Asia, Africa, America and the Islands of the Sea*. In the book's preface, Clayton explains his whereabouts while Johnson fought the death sentence he had imposed: "In 1888, I made an extended tour of Europe, from Sicily to the North Cape and from Paris to Constantinople. The letters of this series give faithful pictures, as far as I was able to paint them, of my experiences and observations during six months of the most active and, to me, most interesting period of my life."

Finally, in September 1888, Clayton was back on the bench, and John B. Robinson—now aided by attorney C. Oscar Beasley—applied for a writ of habeas corpus for Christopher Chopaz, Brinton Walton and Charles Wilson. On September 21, the men were brought from Eastern State Penitentiary to the jail in Media for a preliminary hearing on the charge of murder. Their defense counsel was none other than former district attorney Jesse M. Baker.

Rather than in a courtroom, the hearing was held in jail cell number seventy-one. Lawyers, witnesses, officers and the three prisoners all sat around a long, unpainted table. Wilson's tall, broad frame swallowed the caned chair in which he sat. His arms remained folded across his midsection for most of the proceedings. The flat-topped, wool smoking cap he wore hung on the back of his head, exposing his face and large forehead. He frequently laughed at testimony that amused him and held a firm gaze on whoever was speaking. Chopaz, clearly more unnerved by the hearing, maintained the same guarded expression for most of its length. Brinton Walton, a small man with a stubbly beard and thick mustache, seemed to regard his appearance as an enjoyable respite from the solitary confinement imposed at Eastern State.

As had been the case in Samuel Johnson's trial, the entrance of Susan Sharpless was met by hushed silence. It was obvious she had been crying, and she seemed to wither under the prospect of testifying yet again about the terrible events surrounding her husband's death. Wilson, whose eyes never left the Quaker woman's face, rose to let her pass by him.

Again Susan was asked to describe the man who'd entered her home the night of the murder. She repeated the same description, which by now must have been as familiar as a daily prayer: tall, of good build, frock coat, clothes neither wet nor muddy, spoke indistinctly.

"Do you see anybody in the room that looks like him?" Beasley asked.

Susan looked around the room. She locked eyes with Wilson.

"I don't know," Susan finally replied.

"Which man—Wilson or Chopaz—has a nose more like the man you saw?" the attorney asked, a question to which modern attorneys would vehemently object for its "leading" of the witness's response.

Susan looked at Wilson. "That man's looks more like it."

In a reenactment of Baker's theatrics during the Johnson trial, Beasley put on Wilson's coat and tied a white handkerchief around his own neck. "Does this look like the clothing the man wore?"

Susan said it was similar.

And then Beasley asked a question that had not been asked in any previous arraignment, hearing or trial: "Do you have a safe in your house, Mrs. Sharpless?"

Susan said she did and, prompted by Beasley, offered a description of it.

"Is there anything of value in this safe?"

HIS IDENTITY DOUBTED.

PROBABLE DISCHARGE OF THE ALLEGED MURDERER OF SHARPLESS.

PHILADELPHIA, Dec. 23.—By order of Chief of Police Stewart, Samuel Johnson, the negro who is accused of the murder of John Sharpless, was taken from his cell at the Thirtieth District Station House this afternoon, and securely handcuffed. Special Officer Alexander gripped his arm and led him down the stone steps of the station house to where a patrol wagon was in waiting. Entering it they were driven rapidly to the Broad-street station. A curious crowd was in waiting at the station to get a glimpse of the alleged murderer. The pair boarded the 3:22 train for Media, reaching the sleepy old town at 4:15. The Warden of the Delaware County Jail was in waiting at the station with a wagon to convey him to the jail. Nearly everybody in Media knew that Johnson was coming, but his arrival created no excitement. Media people believe Johnson is an innocent man, and it will be impossible to impanel a Delaware County jury that will hang him on the so-called evidence that Lieut. Roche and Special Officer Alexander have piled up against him. Johnson looked very little like a murderer yesterday, when he was ushered into his new home, which he will, in all probability, occupy until next March, when the court convenes, unless a Justice of the Peace should in the meantime discharge him.

When he is brought out for a hearing Johnson will be arraigned before a Justice, and Jane Pratt and Mrs. Sharpless will be confronted with him. The action of the Justice will depend in a great measure on their testimony. If they fail to identify Johnson as the man who entered the Sharpless house twice on the night of the murder, before and after the deed was committed, the case virtually falls to the ground. Mrs. Sharpless is still much prostrated, and the least excitement discomposes her. Her friend and counsel, Judge Browall, has had several conversations with her about Johnson, and she persists that he is not the murderer. "He does not answer the description at all," said Judge Browall to-day, "and Mrs. Sharpless is convinced that he could not disguise himself to resemble the man."

The New York Times

Immediately after Samuel Johnson's arrest, newspapers ran articles bemoaning the poor and insufficient evidence against him. This *New York Times* article is quite unambiguous about its feelings toward Lieutenant Roche and Special Officer Alexander.

94

"Yes," said Susan. "Bonds and other items."

The justice hearing the testimony quickly determined that sufficient evidence existed to call a grand jury. On September 26, true bills were found against Chopaz and Wilson, but Brinton was sent back to Eastern State exonerated of any involvement in the killing of John Sharpless. The *New York Times*, in its coverage of the grand jury's findings, reported, "The Board of Pardons will no doubt reprieve Johnson, who was to be hanged October 12, until the trial of the two men indicted today shall have taken place."

The pair continued serving the sentences Judge Clayton had handed them in 1886 while awaiting trial for the Sharpless murder. Shortly after it commenced on December 10, 1888, Christopher "Dutch Gus" Chopaz made a shocking confession. He was present, he said, when John Sharpless was murdered, but taking his life was never their intent. According to Chopaz, he and Wilson went to the home to steal the $7,000 supposedly kept in the safe. The job went bad, he explained, when Wilson struck and killed John Sharpless.

Samuel Johnson's release now seemed a foregone conclusion. Chopaz admitted that he and Wilson were the men at the Sharpless homestead that November night in 1885. Samuel Johnson was not with them. Johnson was, therefore, an innocent man.

But after allowing his client to offer this devastating testimony, former district attorney Baker made a startling claim. The Delaware County grand jury that indicted his client, he asserted, had been illegally drawn. His clients, Baker said, were not formally informed of the charges against them prior to the grand jury being convened. It was a small administrative oversight but a technicality other lawyers and defendants had also used to their benefit. A long round of arguments ensued, both sides adamant in the supremacy of their views. In the end, Judge Clayton came down in favor of the defendants. The indictments against Chopaz and Wilson were quashed. Samuel Johnson would remain in jail—the only convicted killer of John Sharpless.

Shortly after this disappointing turn of events, attorney John B. Robinson responded to claims published by the Philadelphia newspaper the *North American*. Robinson insisted that he had neither lost hope for Johnson nor planned to withdraw from his case.

CHAPTER 11

From Death to Life

The power to pardon precedes Pennsylvania's first state constitution. The 1681 charter granted by Charles II to William Penn gave Penn autonomy to pardon all crimes except murder and treason. Criminals charged with these offenses could be reprieved only if it suited the wishes of the king.

By 1838, the governor's constitutional authority became all encompassing. He had unlimited power to intercede in all legal proceedings except impeachment. But as John Dalberg-Acton famously said, "Power tends to corrupt, and absolute power corrupts absolutely." In 1872, after numerous allegations of the abuse of the power of the pardon, the constitution was amended to allow for the creation of a Board of Pardons. No longer would one man be the sole arbiter of life or death. While current law requires unanimous agreement of the board before recommending to the governor a commutation of the death sentence, during the Johnson hearings only a simple majority was necessary.

Most of the case files in the board's archives are thin, containing only several pages of correspondence and decisions. The Johnson file is by contrast substantial, a full two inches thick. On numerous occasions between 1886 and 1887, the Board of Pardons turned down Johnson's request for a commutation of his death sentence but nonetheless granted reprieves from the gallows. These legal notices are all included in the file, but the bulk of the contents are far more personal and compelling. Most of the communications are handwritten, but a rare few are typed. Letters from acquaintances, former governors, would-be investigators, members of the clergy and men and women driven to intervene in the case of a man they'd never met are all saved. The universal sentiment expressed by all writers was the great fear that the death sentence might be imposed on a man undeserving of its cruel and irrevocable finality. The November 5, 1887 letter of Henry C. Snowden, chairman of Delaware County's Board of Charities, effectively summarized the majority view:

> *The announcement just made that the Board of Pardons has refused to interfere in the case of Samuel Johnson, convicted of the crime of murder, is a great shock to a very large number of thoughtful people in this community, who have the gravest doubts of his guilt. While the execution of this man at any time under such circumstances would be looked upon with horror by at least half of our people, to hang him a few days after this adverse decision, without affording him time to prepare for death, would be deemed barbarous.*

But it was not just the Board of Pardons and Governor Beaver who received letters pleading for the life of Samuel Johnson. Beaver's wife, Mary Allison, also received correspondence from women hoping to influence the governor by arousing the sympathies of his gentler half. One such letter included an unsourced newspaper clipping that read:

> *In October 1883 a harness was stolen in North Haven, Conn., and was found in the possession of Charles E. Sparks. He claimed to have bought it, but was convicted of theft, sentenced to the state prison for three years, and served his time out. Frank Hicks, who is dying in Claremont, Mass., has just written a letter confessing that he stole the harness and sold it to Sparks for $12.50.*

Mrs. Penrose, author of the letter, drew a comparison between Sparks—who had unjustly lost three years of his life—and Samuel Johnson, against whom, she asserted, "no Positive Evidence could be found." Penrose went on to warn Mrs. Beaver that if innocent and executed nonetheless, Samuel Johnson would "call from the grave and haunt his executioners." The letter closed with the writer's fervent wish that "God help your husband to perform a Christian act."

Pressure on the board intensified as the accuracy and motivation behind the testimony of Alexander Pritchett and the arresting officers came

John's brother, George Sharpless, and George's wife, Hannah. *Images taken from* A History of Delaware County and Its People.

increasingly under question. Other facts, too, were surfacing. Odd incidents befell the victim's family, which served only to exacerbate the community's disdain of Samuel Johnson's rapid conviction. John Sharpless's relatives were receiving threatening, anonymous letters. The barn of John's brother George was set afire not once but twice, leading many to worry that perhaps the true perpetrators of the crime were sending a very clear message: let the case rest or else.

In January 1888, the *North American* ran an editorial echoing what many observers of the case now felt:

> *The evidence upon which* [Samuel Johnson] *was convicted was far from unquestionable. The testimony upon which the indictment was found was remarkably scaly. The witness Pritchett is said to be a thief and a companion of disreputable characters. By the record he is a convicted thief, a highway robber, and is charged with perjury. Yet upon his testimony Johnson*

was convicted. The Judge charged the jury that if they believed Pritchett they must convict, and if they disbelieved him they must acquit. The case against Johnson is thus narrowed down to close limits. It is known that Pritchett's arraignment for highway robbery was postponed, as Johnson's counsel say, in order to permit him to testify against Johnson.

By what rule of justice is the life of a man jeopardized by the unsupported testimony of a thief and a robber? From the beginning and throughout there appears to have been a concerted effort to make out a case against Johnson by somebody, whether for the glory of doing it or for the reward does not appear clear. But we protest against the hanging of any man to vindicate the theory of a detective or any other person who constructs a theory and then seeks to bend alleged facts to the theory.

It is said that Johnson is a disreputable person, which may well enough be true, but it is no less true that many of the persons who swore against him bear much worse reputations than he has borne. But we do not hang men because they are disreputable merely, because if we did, there would be too few days in any year for the hangman.

If the testimony of disreputable persons be eliminated from the case against Johnson it has not a leg to stand upon. He was not identified as the man who called John Sharpless from his house on the fatal night, and his counsel expect to show that he was not in the neighborhood at that time. If that be proved, he must go free.

Like John M. Broomall earlier, the newspaper had hit on a key problem with the case against Johnson: the substantial reward money offered by the family, the county and other organizations. Its existence made it impossible to determine if testimony was honest or elicited by greed. No one's motives were more blurred than those of Special Officer Thomas Alexander, who was accused by his fellow policeman with taking credit for arrests he did not make for the sole purpose of collecting bounties.

Where the Sharpless case was concerned, Alexander's requests for the $500 offered by the Delaware County commissioners began immediately after Johnson's arrest in Philadelphia in December 1885. A year later, he was one of four claimants petitioning the commissioners for the money, another of whom was also a police officer. Officer Riggs of North Chester Borough was represented by none other than Johnson's attorney John B. Robinson. This conflict of interest did not deter Robinson from arguing that since Riggs was the first to tell Chief Williamson that Johnson should be considered a suspect in the Sharpless case, he, and only he, was entitled to the reward.

But Special Officer Alexander stuck to the story that informant Pritchett had given him Johnson's name two weeks earlier than Riggs reported it to Williamson; therefore, his claim carried precedence.

The hearing lasted four hours, after which the commissioners still made no determination. Although they planned to announce their decision the following Saturday, in actuality it took nearly four years for the commissioners to finally decide that Alexander was indeed entitled to the full $500.

As others profited from Johnson's conviction, public sentiment against it grew stronger. Very little felt right about the arrest and trial of Samuel Johnson—not the questionable ethics of the police, not the hunger of the press for exclusive stories with salacious headlines, not the testimony of convicted criminals and greedy acquaintances. Even the efforts of Johnson's defense attorneys seemed insufficient when the hanging of a man was a very real and likely outcome of the case. And on top of all this, anyone who could read a newspaper knew that two other men, Christopher Chopaz and Charlie Wilson, had also been indicted for the murder and only by means of a legal technicality avoided conviction. It was time for Pennsylvania's Board of Pardons to offer Johnson a chance at freedom or publicly present to the community at large its reasons for failing to do so.

In February 1888, Robinson, Beasley and Cummins again appeared before the board. Johnson's was the fourteenth of fourteen hearings scheduled for the day, and the case was not called until well after ten o'clock in the evening. Beasley argued that reliable witnesses had now been uncovered who could account for Johnson's whereabouts the night of the murder. He impressed on the board that Carrie Lane, now dying, had never changed her story that Johnson spent that night at her home. He implored the members of the board to question where Pritchett got the facts of his testimony and asked them to view it for what it was: false and convenient. It was after midnight when Beasley concluded his comments by reminding the board that "the execution of an innocent man is a thought from which the human mind shrinks in horror." When Beasley finished speaking, Robinson asked for a postponement of the remainder of the hearing until the morning. The board denied the request, and Jesse M. Baker spoke briefly for the commonwealth, mostly taking umbrage with the claims that witnesses were encouraged to present false testimony to abet a quick conviction. All parties present knew he referred to Pritchett.

The board reconvened the next morning without Baker, who returned to Media on an early train. Robinson, in one final attempt to influence their decision, told the board members that the death penalty was particularly absurd in the case of John Sharpless's murder in light of the fact that the citizens of Delaware County—one-third of whom were Quaker—vehemently opposed capital punishment.

Four days later, the Board of Pardons returned their decision. There were, they said, no grounds on which they could intervene in Samuel Johnson's sentence.

The outcry over the perceived absurdity of the board's decision echoed throughout southeastern Pennsylvania. In March 1888, the board received a letter from men whose weighty opinions it could not ignore:

> *Having strong doubts in our own minds as to the question whether Samuel Johnson is in reality the murderer of John Sharpless, we earnestly petition your excellency to grant a further reprieve to this condemned man, in the hope which we cherish that additional evidence may yet be brought to light which will the more conclusively establish the question of either his guilt or innocence.*
>
> *With the strongest abhorrence of the commission of so foul a crime, and desirous that the justice of the law may be vindicated in its sure punishment, we feel that withal a stay of proceedings in this case will neither defeat justice, but rather serve to defend our Commonwealth from the imputation of a possible injustice which may have unwittingly been done to an innocent person.*

This typed correspondence was signed by former Pennsylvania governors James Pollock (at whose suggestion "In God We Trust" is stamped on U.S. coins) and Henry Martyn Hoyt, noted manufacturer Thomas G. Hood and George H. Stuart, philanthropist leader of the American YMCA movement. At the bottom of the letter, in his own hand, appears a postscript from famed retailer and future U.S. postmaster general John Wanamaker that read, "I feel justified in asking the governor for a further reprieve."

In April 1888, the case again came before the board. This time, in addition to his attorneys, Philadelphia detective James I. Donaghy (who had led the raid on the Fernwood Gang), now ex–police chief Williamson and George H. Stuart appeared in support of Johnson. Robinson produced a lead pipe found in the possession of Dutch Gus Chopaz—a weapon that would produce the exact kind of injury suffered by John Sharpless. Williamson and Donaghy offered additional testimony supporting the theory that the Fernwood Gang had indeed killed the Quaker. The men were astounded and enraged when the board said that it would take this new evidence under advisement but offered no decision with regards to Johnson's sentence.

Another year passed. By now, newspapers across the country were openly reporting that other men, not Samuel Johnson, had perpetrated the murder of the wealthy Delaware County Quaker. Men and woman of good conscience were dumbfounded as to how Johnson could possibly still face the threat of hanging.

Perhaps to avoid further public scrutiny, in April 1889 the Board of Pardons held a closed session to discuss the Johnson case. It adjourned without announcing action. But five days later, Governor Beaver received a report that began, "We the undersigned members of the Board of Pardons having carefully considered the application for commutation of Samuel Johnson, who was convicted of murder in the first degree

Top: Famed retailer and future U.S. postmaster general John Wanamaker was but one of the significant men of the day who expressed grave doubts over Samuel Johnson's conviction. *Image courtesy of the Library of Congress.*

Right: Former governor Henry M. Hoyt signed a letter to the Board of Pardons seeking a commutation of Samuel Johnson's sentence. *Image courtesy of the Library of Congress.*

in the court of oyer and terminer of Delaware County, and, on the 6th day of December, 1886, was sentenced by the court to be hanged, do recommend that the said sentence to be hanged be commuted to imprisonment for life."

After more than three years of legal wrangling and 1,500 pages of testimony, the Board of Pardons finally concluded that

> shown by the petitions and letters of men of this state of highest standing and greatest intelligence, and by numerous petitions filed with the board, embracing the names of nearly five thousand citizens, that a very serious and widespread doubt of the prisoner's guilt has been produced in the state, and, with a large number of people, this doubt has grown to a conviction of his innocence. The board are convinced that this feeling is so strong that the execution of the sentence as imposed in this case would produce a moral shock on the minds of many people and be regarded as judicial murder.

The board was largely swayed by letters of men like Senator Thomas V. Cooper, who wrote:

> My first impression was that Johnson had been properly convicted as one of the parties implicated in the murder of John Sharpless, but that he surely had one or more confederates. Subsequent developments have strengthened the belief that more than one man committed the crime. Indeed, I no longer regard any other theory as reasonable. Nothing has been developed to show that Johnson ever had confederates in his many thefts and small robberies, while newly discovered evidence points, with some directness, to well-known criminals who operated in no other way, and one of whom was near the scene of the murder the fatal night. If the newly accused had been tried as early as Johnson was, and with the evidence since gathered as impressively presented, it is not improbable that conviction of some of the Fernwood Gang would have followed.

Like John Y. Worrall, the foreman of the jury during Johnson's murder trial, the Board of Pardons appeased its own conscience by leaving the determination of Johnson's final adjudication to its chief executive. "The commutation of this penalty to imprisonment for life," their report to Governor Beaver concluded, "imposes a punishment regarded in many states fully commensurate to the crime committed, and still leaves it in the power of the executive to interpose a saving hand in case, hereafter, such additional facts shall be shown as to satisfy him beyond a doubt that the prisoner is not guilty."

While Johnson's supporters celebrated, a small few felt that he had quite literally gotten away with murder. An editorial in the June 1, 1889 issue of the *Altoona Mirror* said the fight for Johnson's reprieve was born of "an old political feud of Delaware County"—a clear reference to the animosity between Clayton and Broomall—and described the effort as degrading the administration of justice. It further stated that the evidence against the Fernwood Gang "did not even furnish probable cause for further judicial inquiry." The only logical purpose of the Board of Pardons, the editorial concluded, was to abolish capital punishment in Pennsylvania.

Not surprisingly, African Americans viewed Samuel Johnson's trial as one more wound on the long list of injustices perpetrated on black defendants. Their anger over his treatment remained unabated in 1890, when the Johnson case became something of a rallying cry during the election for representative of the Third District of Philadelphia. Richard Vaux, a white candidate with unvarnished views toward the black residents he supposedly represented, was defeated largely because of the collective opposition of African Americans. They remembered Vaux's reported response when a committee of black men visited him to request assistance in freeing Johnson. "Let them hang him," Vaux told Johnson's supporters. "There'll be one nigger less." Ironically, Vaux served as an inspector of the Eastern State Penitentiary prior to Johnson's incarceration there.

CHAPTER 12

Ten Years, Six Months, Nine Days

In colonial days, Pennsylvania's prisons served as holding tanks for debtors and those facing trial. Groups of prisoners shared cells. Alcohol was sold to inmates, ironically at prices higher than those paid by the non-incarcerated general public. Those who committed serious offenses were conspicuously absent, for they were (often hastily) executed.

By the late eighteenth century, nearly everyone agreed that reforms to the prison system were necessary. Largely through the efforts of the Quakers and the Philadelphia Society for Alleviating the Miseries of Public Prisons, all previous penal laws were repealed in 1790. A new system combining punishment and labor was adopted. Distribution of intoxicating liquors to prisoners was prohibited, untried prisoners and debtors were separated from convicts and prisoners were segregated by gender and age. Inmates received food, clothing and religious instruction. By 1794, the death penalty was enforced only in cases of first-degree murder. The "Pennsylvania system," as it came to be known, combined hard labor with solitary confinement during which prisoners could contemplate and repent their criminal past.

The Pennsylvania legislature passed Act 23, "An Act to Reform the Penal Laws of this Commonwealth," in April 1829. Specifically, the law required that prisoners be kept singularly and separately at labor and in their cells. Wholesome food "of a coarse quality," sufficient for support of life as well as suitable clothes were to be provided. During their confinement "no access shall be had to them by any person or persons" with the exceptions of prison, court or other personnel.

Even the exterior of Eastern State Prison was designed to deter the criminal activity that might land perpetrators behind its walls in solitary confinement. *Image courtesy of Eastern State Penitentiary.*

Compliance with this legislation was taken to its extreme at Eastern State Penitentiary, which, when first opened, offered sufficient facilities to house 250 prisoners. So serious about punishment were its designers that even the exterior—remarkably similar to today's quintessential "haunted castle"—was intended to deter those viewing it from breaking the law. Prisoners wore masks when transported from cells to other areas so as not to make eye contact with guards or fellow inmates. Meals were passed through small openings in cell doors. Each cell had its own small recreation yard. Whether working or sitting idle, prisoners spent their time alone. This would not be problematic, it was guaranteed, so long as there was work for the prisoners to do. Solitary confinement without labor produced insanity, legislators and prison staff agreed. Solitary confinement *with* labor produced moral reform.

Early on, religious and social organizations raised doubts about the efficacy of solitary confinement as a means of rehabilitation. Although the administrators of Eastern State felt no such misgivings, the system quickly started to collapse from the inside out. Within three years of its completion,

Eastern State experienced its first escape. Within five years came the first investigation into its methods and fiscal management.

By 1836, thanks to several additions to the original structure, Eastern State had 450 cells and was becoming a popular tourist attraction for both American and foreign visitors. Writer Charles Dickens visited the prison and afterward publicly stated that he found the institution and its methods "cruel and wrong." Prison inspectors, in their annual report, begged to differ with the opinion of Dickens and others of similar thought. "It seems strange," their 1847 report began, "that so much argument should be necessary to convince wise and humane men that it is desirable to prevent the association of criminals during their term of imprisonment." Inspectors were also keen to point out that "separate" did not truly mean "solitary." Eastern State's inmates, the report explained, were visited "as often as is proper" by prison staff, moral instructors, members of the court and others.

Samuel Johnson arrived at Eastern State Penitentiary on June 22, 1889, entering the facility as prisoner number A4945. In the intake register, Johnson was described as having a black complexion, black eyes and black hair. His foot was eleven inches in length, and he had a small scar over his right eye. His mother was still living, although her name was not recorded. Johnson was listed as unmarried, and it was noted that he was illiterate and never attended school.

By the time of his incarceration, several more cellblocks had been added, and the prison population exceeded 1,100. It was a chaotic facility, and many worried that the prisoners engendered greater fear than the guards and administrators. That concern proved to be not without merit.

Numerous scandals rocked the institution. In one case, thousands of the cigars manufactured by the inmates (as part of their education in the trades) were found to lack both "Internal Revenue" and "inmate made" stamps. Presumably, inmates were selling them directly to customers both in and outside the penitentiary. Unbelievably, during the investigation into the missing cigars, a coin-counterfeiting scheme was uncovered. Although the metals and dyes were seized, there was no way of knowing how many fake dimes, quarters and half dollars had already been manufactured and passed into general currency. Reports poured out of Eastern State about weapons, narcotics and even stills in prisoners' cells. It was like a bad children's fable in which the prisoners were the foxes and the prison staff were the unsuspecting, easily targeted hens.

And yet, as easy as it apparently was to instigate or participate in these illicit enterprises, there are no reports of Samuel Johnson—the petty thief

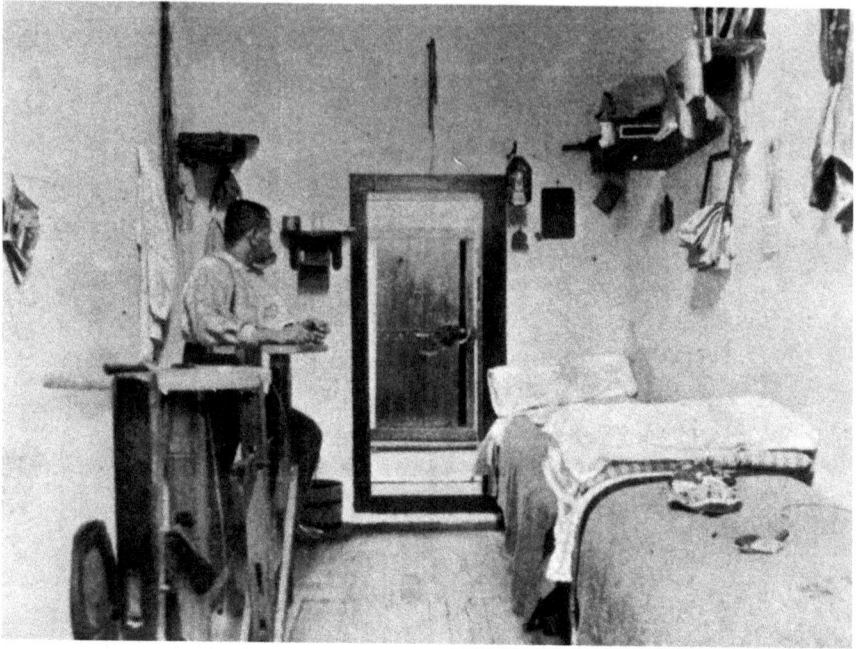

Taken after Eastern State Penitentiary's policy of solitary confinement ceased, this picture shows an inmate wistfully staring at the open cell door. *Image courtesy of Eastern State Penitentiary.*

convicted of cold-blooded murder—involving himself in these schemes. In fact, the very opposite seems true.

Johnson occupied a solitary confinement cell in the prison's first tier. Never in his time at Eastern State did Johnson have a cellmate. George H. Stuart, one of the men who made it his mission to save the prisoner's life, visited Johnson often and likely would have continued had he himself not died in 1890. Few others came after that.

All inmates had a job, and Johnson's was helping with the laundry. He did so without objection or complaint. He never seemed to complain at all. It was the opinion of his keepers at both the Delaware County jail and at Eastern State that Johnson was happy in confinement. There were no decisions for him to make. He had no worries about finding clothing or shelter. And he enjoyed the regular meals. With the exception of several slight attacks of biliousness, Johnson seemed to actually thrive behind bars.

Eastern State Penitentiary ended the year 1899 with a prison population totaling 1,197. On the first day of January 1900, that number dropped by 1.

On New Year's morning, Johnson called a cheery hello to the prison keeper who passed breakfast into his cell. He ate heartily while the keeper continued down the block. A short while later, keeper James Corkin returned with the usual holiday treat of Dutch cake, a simple Pennsylvania German pound cake, and a cup of coffee.

About 10:30 a.m., Corkin passed Johnson's cell once more and observed him sitting on his bed, elbow on the table, forehead resting in his hand. It was a pose the prisoner assumed often, so Corkin initially thought nothing of it. After passing by the cell several more times to see Johnson in this same position, however, Corkin became concerned.

He called Johnson's name. There was no response.

He called again and then a third time. Johnson neither moved nor responded.

Keeper Corkin unlocked the cell and went inside. He gently shook Johnson, but it was obvious there was no further need to try to wake him. Samuel Johnson was dead.

The death of the convicted killer of John Sharpless was covered in newspapers throughout the country. Many reports included the opinion that he had been falsely imprisoned for a murder he did not commit. In one of those strange coincidences one could not purposely contrive, the front-page article about Johnson's death appearing in the *Chester Times* was placed just two columns to the left of a much smaller article entitled "The Clayton Dinner." This short piece spoke of a grand tribute to take place during which the sick and aging judge would receive a large silver service and salutes from most of the lawyers in the county. Clayton passed away less than a month later.

News of Johnson's death saddened acting warden Marvin A. Root. In his daily diary, he wrote:

> *Died, A4945. Samuel Johnson was convicted of murder in Delaware County Court and sentenced to be hung. Sentence was commuted to imprisonment for life by the board of pardons on May 31, 1889. Served ten years, six months and nine days. He was found in a dying condition this morning at 10 o'clock by overseer James Corkin of the Fourth Block. Dr. Goodrich was summoned immediately, it was too late to be of any service. Died of heart disease. His remains will be taken charge of by the coroner. He was a good, quite orderly prisoner.*

Dr. Herbert R. Goodrich, the penitentiary physician, decided after his examination that Johnson likely died of heart disease. Coroner Dugan was then notified. He removed the body to the morgue, where an autopsy

DEATHS WITH CAUSES FOR THE YEAR 1900.

Number	Register No.	Age at Death	Color.	Sex.	Nationality.	Occupation.	Crime.	No. of Convictions.	Condition on Entrance		Cause of Death.	Date of Death		Time Served	
									Physical.	Mental.		M.	D.	Y.	M.	D.
1	A 4945	61	Black.	Male.	Delaware.	Laborer.	Murder.	2	Good.	Degenerate.	Heart Disease.	1	1	10	6	9
2	" 9960	33	White.	"	Philadelphia.	Thief.	Counterfeiting.	1	Phthisis.	Good.	Phthisis.	1	1		6	30
3	" 8787	29	"	"	Italy.	Laborer.	Murder, second degree.	1	Good.	"	Heart Disease.	1	10	2	7	20
4	" 8691	29	"	"	Pennsylvania.	Moulder.	Robbery.	1	Phth. Habit.	"	Phthisis.	2	23	3	10	19
5	B 471	54	"	"	"	Farmer.	Sodomy.	1	Good.	"	Suicide.	3	9			22
6	" 127	43	"	"	"	Thief.	Larceny.	6	Phthisis.	"	Phthisis.	5	20	1		23
7	" 800	68	"	"	New Jersey.	Laborer.	Fel. Entry, Larceny, and Robbery.	1	Morph. Maniac.	"	"	4	12	1	6	8
8	A 9382	37	"	"	Pennsylvania.	Barber.	Larceny.	2	Good.	Degenerate.	Peritonitis.	5	20	2	3	4
9	" 6444	38	"	"	"	Idle.	Murder, second degree.	1	Phthisis.	Good.	Phthisis.	6	30	7	9	6
10	B 188	31	"	"	Germany.	Thief.	Burglary.	3	Good.	"	Peritonitis.	9	30	1	1	25
11	A 8416	53	"	"	Pennsylvania.	Cigar Maker.	Assault and Battery to Kill.	1	Phthisis.	"	Cancer of Penis.	10	16	1	9	24
12	B 72	31	"	:	"	Laborer.	Burglary.	5	Phthisis.	"	Phthisis.	10	16	1	7	22
13	A 8371	53	"	"	New York.	Thief.	Felonious Wounding.	1	Phth. Habit.	"	"	10	23	6		28
14	" 9450	60	"	"	"	Thief.	Receiving Stolen Goods.	4	Senility.	"	Cancer of Pylorus.	11	12	1	11	4
15	" 8799	72	Black.	"	"	Stone Mason.	Burglary, Larceny, and Receiving.	2	"	"	Nephritis.	12	8	4	6	21

Like all prisoner deaths, Samuel Johnson's was recorded in the annual statistical report created and published by the penitentiary. *Taken from the* Annual Report of the Inspectors of Eastern State Penitentiary.

confirmed this was indeed the cause of death. Customarily after an autopsy, family members or friends come to claim the body, but Johnson hadn't been visited in years, and no one could be located who might arrange for his burial. This being the case, Johnson's body was donated to the Anatomical Board.

The Pennsylvania Anatomical Board was created in 1883. Legislation mandated that the board be composed of professors and demonstrators of anatomy and surgery at medical and dental schools around the commonwealth. It was the duty of this board to distribute human bodies to schools that would use them for study and the promotion of medical science.

All public officers and agents of county and local almshouses, morgues, hospitals, prisons and other public facilities were made aware of the board and its purpose. Moreover, these officers and agents were required to immediately notify the Anatomical Board of bodies not claimed by relatives, friends or fraternal societies within twenty-four hours.

If a body was unfit for the board's purpose, the poor director buried it at his own expense. And if a public official failed to deliver a body in time for use in medical study, he bore the cost of burial personally.

Johnson, who in life never possessed the means to contribute to the society around him, at least in death did when his remains became the subject of scientific study. Sadly, however, the corpses obtained by the Anatomical Board at that time received little in the way of burial. Johnson—and other bodies from the Philadelphia area falling under the board's authority—were sent to a memorial park in Montgomery County. What records might have existed were destroyed by fire in 1947, and any markers that might have been placed on these paupers' graves were bulldozed over in a cemetery expansion project.

13174

RETURN OF A DEATH
✦IN THE CITY OF PHILADELPHIA✦

CORONER'S CERTIFICATE.

1. Name of deceased *Samuel Johnson*
2. Color, *Colored.*
3. Sex, *Male*
4. Age, *50 Years*
5. Married or single, *Single*
6. Date of Death, *Jan 1st 1900*
7. Cause of Death, *Heart Disease*

Thomas Dugan Coroner.
Per Edgar

UNDERTAKER'S CERTIFICATE IN RELATION TO DECEASED.

8. Occupation,
9. Place of Birth,
10. When a Minor { Name of Father,
{ Name of Mother,
11. Ward, *15th*
12. Street and Number, *Eastern Penitentiary*
13. Date of Burial, *January 8th 1900*
14. Place of Burial, *Potters Field*

George M. Mathews Undertaker.

Residence, *Coroners Office*

This Constitutes one Certificate, to be returned to the Health Office on Saturday of each week, before 12 M.

Samuel Johnson's death certificate. *From the death records of the City of Philadelphia.*

The Pennsylvania Anatomical Board went on to become the Humanity Gifts Registry. While its function remains the same, those who donate their bodies to education and research are recognized in an annual Celebration of Remembrance. Unlike Samuel Johnson, whose earthly remains disappeared into an eternity of neglect and disrespect, donors to the Humanity Gifts Registry are now documented and honored.

CHAPTER 13
Her Beloved Husband

Samuel Johnson faded from the news almost immediately after the commutation of his life sentence. Once the threat of death passed, it seems there was little impetus to work to actually prove his innocence. Once regularly visited by attorneys, reporters and supporters, Johnson spent nearly his full final decade in prison without seeing anyone from the outside world.

Of course, one tremendous question remains: if Samuel Johnson did not commit the murder, who did? Was it the Fernwood Gang's Charlie Wilson, or was Chopaz simply offering Wilson up as a means to lighten—or evade—his own punishment? There is little doubt that Susan and Jane saw two men that night: one at the door and another inside the home. Was it William T. Colwell, the man with the buck teeth who traveled with a younger companion? As the intruder backed out of the Sharpless home, Susan said his eyes swept continuously from the window to the door. Was the man who kept the women contained in the sitting room looking for his accomplice's signal that the deed was done? We don't know, nor will we ever know who really killed John Sharpless.

John B. Robinson, James S. Cummins and C. Oscar Beasley would be associated with Samuel Johnson for the rest of their lives. Biographical sketches of all three men mention their participation in the case, all of the sketches crediting their subject for saving the life of the "negro Johnson." Beasley went on to serve as a Philadelphia councilman and is widely credited as the driving force behind the construction of the Reading Terminal at Twelfth and Market Streets, which is today part of the Pennsylvania

Convention Center. The market underneath the terminal still operates much as it did in the 1890s.

Thomas Jefferson Clayton, never a man to inspire ambiguous opinions, remained equally controversial in death. One obituary observed that his passing might finally bring harmony to the fractured Delaware County Republican Party. Several death notices mentioned the bitter political battle surrounding his first election to the bench, greatly fueling the legendary war between him and his rival Broomall.

John M. Broomall's death in 1894 was marked by a chorus of mournful praise. The *Titusville Morning Herald* reported that his speech in support of the Thirteenth Amendment was one of the "most magnificent utterances" ever voiced in the U.S. House of Representatives. His view of the evils of capital punishment never wavered. Broomall's friends noted that it was accepted as gospel truth throughout the county that no man could be hanged for murder if he was defended by Judge Broomall.

Although the eventual fate of Special Officer Thomas Alexander is unknown, Lieutenant David Roche was suspended in September 1886 for his part in two horrific attacks perpetrated in Philadelphia—the first on a group of men in a bar on Sixth Street and the second against an apparent stranger unfortunate enough to be walking along Locust Street. Drunken and aided by several others, including a city councilman, a constable and a police sergeant, Roche staggered toward a group of African Americans waiting at the tavern to be served. "You're the niggers that worked for [political candidate] Bruno Ernest, damn you," Roche shouted. "You hadn't ought to vote anyhow!" Roche then drew a revolver and fired indiscriminately at the men, who rushed for the rear door. Sergeant Beatty joined in on the shooting while the rest of the frenzied gang attacked the terrified men with blackjacks. One of Roche's bullets landed in the neck of William Powell. Powell was taken to his home, but police officers appeared shortly thereafter and drove the mortally injured man away in a cab. In a senseless final act, Roche and Councilman John R. Lloyd fell upon a man named Charles Petroff and beat him on the head with blackjacks until he lost consciousness. After a forced leave of absence, Roche was reinstated by Mayor William Burns Smith and resumed his service as lieutenant of the Third District. Finally, in March 1887, he was dismissed by director of public safety William S. Stokely on the order of newly elected mayor Edwin H. Fitler.

Delaware County is today home to more than half a million residents. The Springfield Meetinghouse in which John and Susan married is now the Peace Center of Delaware County. It is still guided by the values inherent in the teachings of the Religious Society of Friends and is steered by a committee that includes a representative of the Springfield Monthly Meeting. It is strongly associated with the peace, justice and environmental movements—priorities that John Sharpless would likely support and admire.

Susan lived her final years with her sister, Jane Pratt, constantly by her side. How many times did they speak of that night in 1885 and the knock on the door that changed everything? How often did they wonder if they could have done something differently—something that might have changed the course of history? Or perhaps they did not speak of the murder at all.

As late as August 1899, the Widow Sharpless still publicly opined that Samuel Johnson was innocent of the murder. This flew in the face of those who long believed she refused to identify Johnson because of her Quaker opposition to capital punishment. Johnson's death sentence had already been commuted. Why would she still lie?

Susan listed herself as "head of household" on the 1900 census and gave her occupation as landlady. Jane was listed as her "companion." By 1910, Jane now gone, Susan was living as a boarder in the home of neighbor Ellis Barker, although she maintained ownership of the Sharpless homestead.

Susan H. Sharpless lived to the esteemed age of ninety-two—a remarkable lifespan matching that of her father. Although confined to her room the last two years of her life, she never lost her mental faculties and remained interested in and abreast of local and national events. She died on September 11, 1917, surviving her younger sister by eight years.

Susan's obituary appeared in the *Chester Times* and, even thirty-two years after the crime, prominently featured her husband's killing. Its headline, in bold type, read, "Death of the Widow of John Sharpless, Who

The historical marker that today sits on the corner of the front lawn of the Chester Meetinghouse. *Photograph taken by the author.*

117

This broken wrought-iron gate used to mark the entrance to the Chester Meetinghouse cemetery where the low, plain stones of the Sharpless family can be found. Buried from left to right are Jane Pratt, Susan H. Sharpless, John Sharpless, their son Martin and John's parents, Ruth and John. *Photographs taken by the author.*

Was Murdered While Doing a Kind Act." The obituary went on to describe the murder as the "one surprise" thrust upon Susan's life, occurring when a "cruel assassin…appeared in the darkness and struck him down." In truth, however, Susan had survived many sad surprises, not the least of which must have been the death of her four-year-old son.

The value of the personal property and real estate owned by Susan at the time of her death totaled just over $39,000, and all of it was distributed to family, friends and the church. Her will was a simple final testament to her generosity and devotion. A $100 bequest was given to the Women's Beneficent Society of Chester; $500 went to the Chester County Monthly Meeting of Friends, where the family worshiped and was buried. Susan specifically asked that her grave, as well as the graves of her husband and son, be perpetually tended. A separate $200 bequest was given for the upkeep of the burial grounds in their entirety. Any surplus from her bequests was to be applied toward the maintenance of neglected graves of the dead forgotten by their own families.

And hidden among the remaining final requests was the brief but telling instruction that John's brother George should receive a shaving glass—a shaving glass that Susan undoubtedly gently cleaned over and over again before placing it back in the same position each time, exactly where John Sharpless had last left it, all the while praying against reason that her beloved husband might return home to use it.

Sources

Annual Report of the Inspectors of the Eastern State Penitentiary for the Eastern District of Pennsylvania for the Year 1900. Philadelphia: Allen, Lane & Scott, 1901.

Ashmead, Henry Graham, and Austin N. Hungerford. *History of Delaware County.* Philadelphia: J.B. Lippincott, 1884.

Clayton, Thomas J. *Rambles and Reflections: Europe from Biscay to the Black Sea and from Aetna to the North Cape with Glimpses at Asia, Africa, America and the Islands of the Sea.* Chester, PA: Delaware County Republican, 1892.

Clemency File. Records of the Department of Justice, Board of Pardons. Pennsylvania State Archives, Record Group 15.

Cope, Gilbert. *Genealogy of the Sharpless Family: Descended from John and Jane Sharpless, Settlers near Chester, Pennsylvania, 1682.* Philadelphia: Sharpless Bicentennial Committee, 1887.

Delaware County, Pennsylvania. Orphans Court Records.

———. Register of Wills Records.

Delaware County Tax Assessment Records, 1791–1848. Pennsylvania State Archives, Records Group 47.

Futhey, J. Smith, and Gilbert Cope. *History of Chester County with Genealogical and Biographical Sketches.* Philadelphia: Louis H. Everts, 1881.

Griffiths, Ralph, and George Edward Griffiths. *Monthly Review: or Literary Journal Enlarged* (September 1866).

Hopkins, Henry W. *Atlas of Delaware County, Pennsylvania.* Philadelphia: G.M. Hopkins, 1870.

Jordan, John W. *Colonial and Revolutionary Families of Pennsylvania.* New York: Lewis Publishing Company, 1911.

Journal of the Common Council of the City of Philadelphia. Vol. 1. Philadelphia: Dunlap & Clarke, 1886.

Journal of Prison Discipline and Philanthropy 40 (January 1901).

Marriage and Divorce, 1867–1906. Vol. 1, Special Reports. Department of Commerce and Labor, United States Bureau of the Census.

Martin, John Hill. *Chester (and Its Vicinity) Delaware County in Pennsylvania.* Philadelphia: Wm. H. Pike & Sons, 1877.

Official Documents Comprising the Department and Other Reports Made to the Governor, Senators and House of Representatives of Pennsylvania. Vol. 1, Report of the Board of Pardons. 1892.

Patent Index, A and AA Series, 1684–1781. Records of the Land Office. Pennsylvania State Archives, Record Group 17.

Portrait and Biographical Record of Lancaster County, Pennsylvania. Chicago: Chapman Publishing Co., 1894.

Prison Administration Records. Records of the Department of Justice, Eastern State Penitentiary. Pennsylvania State Archives, Record Group 15.

Prison Population Records. Records of the Department of Justice, Eastern State Penitentiary. Pennsylvania State Archives, Record Group 15.

Records of the Friends Burial Grounds, Twenty-fourth and Chestnut Street. Chester, Pennsylvania.

Scharf, John Thomas. *History of Delaware: 1609–1888.* Philadelphia: L.J. Richards & Co., 1888.

Sharpless, Isaac. *Two Centuries of Pennsylvania History.* Philadelphia: J.B. Lippincott Co., 1900.

Smith, George, M.D. *History of Delaware County, Pennsylvania, from the Discovery of the Territory Included within Its Limits to the Present Time.* Philadelphia: Henry B. Ashmead, 1862.

Sprogle, Howard O. *The Philadelphia Police, Past and Present.* Philadelphia, 1887.

Weekly Notes of Cases Argued and Determined in the Supreme Court of Pennsylvania, the County Courts of Philadelphia, and the United States District and Circuit Courts for the Eastern District of Pennsylvania. Vol. 20. Philadelphia: Kay & Brother, 1888.

NEWSPAPERS

Space constraints prohibit the listing of every one of the hundreds of newspaper articles consulted while researching this book. Suffice it to say, however, that the facts and contextual details offered by these stories provided an immeasurable understanding of the time and place in which the killing of John Sharpless occurred. What follows is a list, organized by state, of the most pertinent publications on which the author relied.

Maryland
Baltimore American
New York
New York Age
New York Times
Utica Herald
World

Pennsylvania
  Altoona Mirror
  Chester Times
  Delaware County American
  Delaware County Republican
  Gettysburg Star & Sentinel
  Greenville Advance Argus
  Lebanon Daily News
  New Oxford Item
  North American [Philadelphia]
  Philadelphia Record
  Pittsburgh Dispatch
  Sentinel & Republican [Mifflintown, PA]

Two Quaker publications of immense assistance were *Friends Intelligencer and Journal* and the *Friend.*

About the Author

If you include her third-grade poem published by the *Hummelstown Sun*, Stephanie has been working as a published writer since 1967. Traditionalists, however, would likely say that Stephanie's professional writing career began in 1984, when she was hired as a stringer by the long-defunct *Pennsylvania Beacon*. Since that time, she has amassed more than two hundred bylines in local, regional and national publications and has conducted historical and genealogical research for nearly two thousand clients.

A lifelong Pennsylvania resident born within smelling distance of the Hershey Chocolate Factory, Stephanie specializes in topics relating to the Keystone State. *The Killing of John Sharpless* is her first book and encompasses all three of Stephanie's passions: Pennsylvania, history and true crime.

Stephanie lives in the Capital Region of the state with her husband, two dogs, two cats (the brains of the operation) and an adult son who "moved out" but returns regularly for dinners and to do a quick load of whites. When not writing or researching for editors or paying clients, she writes and researches *Hauntingly PENNSYLVANIA™*, her own history site, for free.

Stephanie enjoys compliments, so if you have any to share about *The Killing of John Sharpless*, please contact her via her website, StephanieHoover.com.

Visit us at
www.historypress.net
....
This title is also available as an e-book